What the Experts Are Saying about
Stop Fighting Over the Kids

"STOP Fighting Over the Kids will become a classic, to be added to the shelves of all professionals who work with separating and divorcing families. It is a personal and comprehensive work that is both inspirational and practical. Attorney Mastracci pulls no punches. Speaking directly to parents, he reminds them of their highest obligation: to keep their children safe, secure, well cared for, and healthy. This no-nonsense and sometimes colorful approach is effective because he weaves his personal experiences with his professional ones; every word hits the right note. The lists of Dos and Don'ts at the end of most chapters make for easy reference guides for parents. I can see myself printing out some of those lists for clients; they are that practical and realistic. Buy this book by the dozen and start handing it out to your clients now.

—Attorney Rita S. Pollak, Past-President of the
International Academy of Collaborative Professionals (IACP),
Past President of the Massachusetts Collaborative Law Council (MCLC),
and Past President of the Massachusetts chapter of the
Association of Family and Conciliation Courts (AFCC).
www.collaborativpractice.com

"Mike Mastracci's book is the best I have ever seen for people who are heading for separation and possible divorce and for those who are already divorced and struggling with shared parenting issues. Every important potential problem is discussed in a straightforward manner and every issue comes with practical, clearly written, and do-able recommendations for their solution. In my professional opinion, every recommendation for children is consistent with what we know is important for their emotional health and well-being.

The author clearly explains why litigation should be a last resort and offers practical steps to avoid it. Mastracci also helps readers understand what can and cannot be expected of courts and judges. Not only is this book a great source for those personally struggling with these issues, but it can serve as an excellent source book for mental health professionals working in the area as well as students of all disciplines interested in family law."

—Leon A. Rosenberg, Ph.D., Professor Emeritus Counseling, Psychiatry, and Pediatrics of the Johns Hopkins University and the Johns Hopkins School of Medicine. [He currently serves as a consultant in the Division of Child and Adolescent Psychiatry at the Johns Hopkins Hospital. Dr. Rosenberg maintains a private practice specializing in consultation to attorneys and families in matters of divorce, custody, abuse and neglect, and protection of children and the protection of parental rights.]

"*STOP Fighting Over the Kids* is a must for parents contemplating separation and divorce and all professionals who work with families in transition. Being honest about his own family transition, Mike Mastracci provides a how-to guide to help parents address the needs of their children. Mike found "Big Rock" — his center — his spiritual place that he shared with his son. He invites us all, particularly parents, to find their own rocks to help them through and keep the focus of all decisions on the real best interests of their children. At the same time, Mike addresses all professionals, judges, attorneys, mediators, and mental health professionals working with families, challenging us to take the highest road for children. His discussion of collaborative law is particularly meaningful. Collaborative law builds a lasting road map for parents and provides an active voice for children so that their developmental needs are heard and addressed. It is time for each of us who works with families and is part of a family to define what children really need in order to grow and thrive. Mike Mastracci has accomplished this in his book and in his wonderful relationship with his son, which is the best testimony to taking the high road that Mike advocates for all of us."

—Risa Garon, LCSW-C, BCD, CFLE
Executive Director, National Family Resiliency Center
www.DivorceABC.com

"This easy-to-read book is jam-packed with insights, information, and guidance — the likes of which I have yet to see anywhere else. As a Certified Family Law Specialist in California and an attorney practicing custody litigation for over 27 years, I have, quite literally, seen it all in child custody disputes. Mastracci has created a resource that I plan on sending my clients. *STOP Fighting Over the Kids* should be required reading for anyone with children, whether divorce or custody litigation is looming in their future or not. This is a valuable read for parents, period. It helps us to understand the depths of the emotions and consequences that our behavior as adults and parents in these difficult situations can have on our children. The resources the author provides are clear and even-handed. He has created a roadmap for successful parenting that should become a staple in every custody lawyer's library and a recommended resource on every courthouse website. I will continue to refer to and recommend this invaluable resource. It is replete with personal candor, wisdom, and guidance. *STOP Fighting Over the Kids* has already helped me as a parent and as a custody lawyer."

—Marshal W. Waller, Certified Family Law Specialist
Dr. Phil's "Best of the Best" Child Custody Attorney
Feinberg & Waller
www.feinbergwaller.com

"Divorce in the 21st century is devolving into a shipwreck of relationships with children as the unintended, unsuspecting victims. Enter now a "Beacon of Light" from collaborative divorce attorney Mike Mastracci, who provides us with a caring, clear, concise manual describing the steps to follow in a marital separation or divorce to protect children and parents from myriad emotional and common pitfalls. *STOP Fighting Over the Kids* is also an extremely valuable and welcome addition to any psychologist's available resources."

—Michael L. Boyle, Ph.D., clinical psychologist,
Co-founder of the Mediation Center, Ellicott City, Maryland

"This book is a must-read for every parent, grandparent, and friend of the family that is involved in a custody battle. Attorney Mastracci has done a masterful job of providing sane, sensible, and fair advice that has the best interests of the child at heart while looking out for the needs of both parents."

—Arielle Ford, Author
The Soulmate Secret

"*STOP Fighting Over the Kids* provides the tools, resources, and insight that every divorcing parent needs. You will learn how to promote and foster the right mindset from someone who has "walked the walk." This book is excellent, especially for those who are serious about keeping their children out of the middle of parental conflicts."

—Raoul Felder, Celebrity Divorce Lawyer
www.raoulfelder.com

STOP Fighting Over the Kids is a clear and comprehensive guide based on this caring attorney's years of experience dealing with divorce "wars." His advice is sound, compassionate, and valuable for any parent facing the challenges of divorce. If you want to protect your children in the best possible way, I highly recommend this. book."
—Rosalind Sedacca, CCT, The Voice of Child-Centered Divorce
Author, *How Do I Tell the Kids about the Divorce?*
A Create-a-Storybook Guide to Preparing Your Children — with Love!
www.childcentereddivorce.com

As co-founder of the Michigan SMILE program, an educational seminar for parents regarding the impact of divorce on children, I was delighted to read Michael Mastracci's Stop Fighting over the Kids. His approach makes it clear that parental conflict can be toxic for children and that every mother and father has the power to minimize that impact by learning and agreeing to put their children first. This book presents a roadmap to make this better outcome possible. I highly recommend it to anyone who wants to take their kids out of the middle and put them on the path to fulfillment of their potential.
—Honorable Edward Sosnick, Circuit Court Judge, Co-founder of the Michigan SMILE Program for Divorcing Families

STOP

Fighting Over the Kids

STOP

Fighting Over the Kids

Resolving Day-to-Day Custody Conflict in Divorce Situations

 Mike Mastracci's
DIVORCE WITHOUT DISHONOR® SERIES

St. Gabriel's Press  Baltimore, MD

STOP Fighting Over the Kids;
Resolving Day-to-Day Custody Conflict in Divorce Situations
by Mike Mastracci
A part of *Mike Mastracci's Divorce Without Dishonor® Book Series*

Published by St. Gabriel's Press, LLC
614 Edmondson Avenue, Baltimore, MD 21228
www.SaintGabrielsPress.com / www.DivorceWithout Dishonor.com
info@SaintGabrielsPress.com

This book is available in volume for qualifying organizations. For more information about this book or Divorce Without Dishonor®, please contact the publisher or
visit www.DivorceWithoutDishonor.com or www.SaintGabrielsPress.com

Cover and interior design by Pneuma Books, LLC
www.pneumabooks.com

Cover photograph courtesy of Jupiter Images

ISBN-13: 978-0-9816310-0-4
ISBN-10: 0-9816310-0-2

Library of Congress Control Number: 2008936874

PRINTED IN THE UNITED STATES OF AMERICA

∞

17 16 15 14 13 12 11 10 09   03 04 05 06 07 08 09 10

DIVORCEWITHOUTDISHONOR.COM

*This book is dedicated to Nicholas, my awesome son,
and to the memory of my grandmother,
our family matriarch:*

*Mary DePersio Mastracci
(August 11, 1900 – January 14, 1992)*

*Though you did not get to see my "main man" while here on earth,
we thank you for always watching over us.*

*With eternal love,
~Mike*

Contents

❦ TABLE OF CONTENTS ❧

Foreword

by David L. Levy, J.D., Board President,
The Children's Rights Council (CRC)

Each year millions of children whose parents are separated, divorced, or never married are placed at risk. Three out of four teenage suicides occur in households where a parent has been absent. More than 80 percent of felons in prison were raised without a father. When you hear of children becoming involved in drugs or crime, dropping out of school, or getting pregnant as teenagers, the odds are more than two to one that these are children raised by single parents.

Single parents are to be commended for all they do for their children. And most single parents would like the other parent to be involved, but more must be done to encourage what has been a historical, cultural, and social norm in virtually every society. A parent is a parent and should be supported as such, but data clearly show that children raised by both mom and dad have an advantage in life. This is not to say that children raised in other family configurations cannot turn out well; they can and they do.

For innumerable reasons, the number of single parents in the United States has increased dramatically since the early 1970s. Research was slow to reveal that children with both a mom and a dad active in their lives actually perform better on every social indicator of childhood behavior. Indeed, it wasn't until the 1990s that research began to show the problematic results of a generation of children raised by single parents; hence, a new reality began to unfold.

To meet these challenges, organizations such as my Children's Rights Council (which actually got its start in 1985) and parent support groups around the country began to emerge. These groups worked to counsel non-custodial parents on how to handle custody, access (visitation), and financial child support issues. Books and research also increasingly focused on parenting topics. Some books dealt with parenting in general, while others focused primarily on the at-risk population of children whose parents are separated, divorced, or never-married.

As head of the Children's Rights Council since its inception, I am familiar with most of the literature. Many of these books are quite good, but I can assure you that Mike Mastracci's *Stop Fighting Over the Kids* is one of the best. It ranks high because the author's twenty-plus years of practicing law and working to help families makes him intimately familiar with the problems facing separated and divorced couples. Furthermore, the process of struggling through his own child custody challenges gave him further depth, experience, empathy, and understanding. If parents have to get divorced, they would do well to read this book before they take a single step in hiring a lawyer or driving to the courthouse. The decisions you make from Step 1 — considering divorce — all the way to raising your children to adulthood and beyond will be enhanced by this book's practical advice and sensible approach.

There is not one step in resolving day-to-day custody conflict that this book does not cover in terms that will help you and the other parent keep your children out of the middle of a custody battle. Be assured that custody battles will harm your children. Your conflict will reach their ears, their minds, and their hearts. It cannot help but make them worry and fret, no matter how hard you try to insulate them from the struggle.

Make your best attempt to put your children first, which will not only lessen their pain, but yours as well. Help yourself to a generous dollop of wisdom that will help you and every member of your family come out as unscarred as possible from what is happening around you. Stop fighting over the kids. Let Mike Mastracci show you how. It will be worth it.

—David L. Levy, J.D., Board President,
The Children's Rights Council (CRC)
www.CRCkids.org

Preface

For years I have searched for a uniquely informative, child-focused, thought-provoking, inspirational, and lightly entertaining book to assist my family law clients in making important changes for themselves, and more importantly, for the innocent victims that they continually fight over and about — their children. When I joined the ranks of the ever growing numbers of separated and divorced parents, I could not find a book that contained what I felt was the right combination of practical, legal, parental, and situational guidance. What follows is the type of empowering information that I wish I had found when I did not know what I know now. I share this information with you for the benefit of your children.

More than a dozen years have passed since my first wife and I separated. Ugly from the start, our divorce was full of prolonged rancor and intense hostility. There was nothing concerning our son that we did not fight over. From where he would live to what pre-school he would attend, it was all up for grabs. It was all one never-ending argument. All of it went to our attorneys, and ultimately, a stranger in a black robe would decide our son's fate.

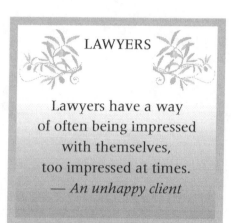

LAWYERS

Lawyers have a way
of often being impressed
with themselves,
too impressed at times.
— *An unhappy client*

The cost? Hundreds of thousands of dollars. That's right. Hundreds of thousands of dollars. Just think of the ways that kind of money could be put to better use. While the financial costs can be devastating, the emotional fallout is usually much worse. Too many children grow up as victims of parental warfare. It needs to stop.

I tell you this simply to let you know that I have been in the trenches both personally and professionally. I am familiar with the feelings, motives, actions, and results of child custody chaos. I have worked as an attorney for nearly twenty years, and I have served as counsel on more than my fair share of divorce and custody cases.

One of the more interesting years of my life was between 1998 and 1999. During that time my ex-wife and I were between round one and the inevitable round two of our court-involved child custody disputes. In those days, I was consumed by the issues of separation, divorce, and child custody problems and solutions. This burning desire led to my organizing, founding, and running Maryland's first full-service Child Access Center. Both then and now, I have great empathy for people who are stuck on the litigation path.

In addition to providing detailed reports and testimony to the courts, the Child Access Center provided a child friendly environment for neutral child pick-ups and drop-offs and offered a comprehensive referral network to suit the needs of families in transition. The center was also used for supervised visitation, parenting classes, and child-related advocacy meetings and seminars. Although the personnel at the center were sympathetic to mothers, fathers, and grandparents alike, the primary focus was on the legal rights of children, as well as their natural rights to enjoy loving relationships with all family members.

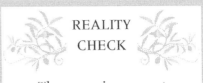

REALITY CHECK

The superior parent must rise above and overcome many obstacles to effectively interact with their children's other parent. This challenge is often the biggest stumbling block to happiness and stability for all concerned.

All of these experiences have taught me what you already know — divorce and custody issues are never easy — but they can be easier. They really can.

As you are learning, a marital separation, and even a final divorce decree, cannot and does not end your responsibility as a parent. Parents are forever. Both parents should make every attempt to be active in the lives of their children. You know that children need constant love, nurturing, and understanding from their parents. You know that it is vital for children to feel that they have parents who love them, even though their parents could not be happy with one another.

Like most people who go through the process of separation and divorce, you are probably experiencing feelings of isolation, despair, anger, depression, loneliness, grief, guilt, and a loss of self-confidence. It is likely that you are worried about many things: the welfare of your children, your finances, a new social life, and the fulfillment of basic human needs. It's a time of uncertainty and up-heaval, but it presents you with a choice. You can use this time as an opportunity for growth or you can surrender to self-pity. The superior parent must rise above and overcome many obstacles to effectively interact with their children's other parent. This challenge is often the biggest stumbling block to happiness and stability for all concerned.

Fortunately, as you will soon see, the ways that divorce cases and child custody and visitation disputes are handled in the legal profession have begun to change in recent years. However, the nature and types of parental disputes that still end up overwhelming our judicial system and disrupting the lives of our children are often part of the same old song and dance.

If you're embroiled in conflict, I want to encourage you as well as assist you in making practical choices that will improve the quality of your life and your children's lives. You can't change your former spouse (you already know that, right?), but you can change you. I've kept it real in this book, and I've addressed the most common problems that separated and divorced parents encounter all the time. After you read this book, you'll have the tools and resources to transform your life while improving the quality of your relationships with your children and their other parent. I guarantee it.

—Mike Mastracci,
www.DivorceWithoutDishonor.com

1

The Path to Big Rock

The day my main man was born in the spring of 1993, I remember walking my parents down to their car to say goodbye. We were all holding back happy tears. After hugging my father, I told him that I hoped that I could be half as good a father to Nicholas as he has been to me. His eyes filled up, he grabbed my shoulders, and he gently shook me and said, "Son, do you know that is exactly what I said to my father the day you were born?" What a moment!

Nicholas and I bonded like I could never have imagined. I was in awe. I still am. I have a son. I am someone's daddy — his hero. What an awesome feeling. What an awesome responsibility. What a blessing. I love him with all my heart.

Within two years of the birth of my son, my love for our child, my heart and soul, would be put to the test. My wife and I were divorcing and we declared war over the future of our son and our respective lives with him. Our ideas about the way things would be after our separation and divorce were in direct conflict. The resulting years of litigation, the hundreds of thousands of dollars spent on lawyers' fees and related costs as well as the emotional up-

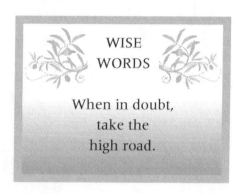

WISE WORDS

When in doubt, take the high road.

heavals that came with the struggles took their toll on us all. We did it the hard way. It was an all out parental war, and it changed my life, forever.

Throughout the whirlwind of it all, nestled in the woods of a nearby state park, a large rock became my bunker. Although it appeared to be nothing more than a huge boulder, it somehow became a source of inner strength for me. My son named it "Big Rock."

We hiked there often with binoculars, backpack, and picnic lunch, and I would feel a temporary sense of peace and tranquility. Those hikes along the high road were necessary respites from the parental arms race that his mother and I had quickly let take on a life of its own. To Nicholas, an innocent child, we were journeying deep into the jungle looking for wild animals. We would climb high atop Big Rock where we kept an eye out for Bambi and other animals. It was our special place. Fortunately, those father-son experiences meant as much to Nicholas as they did to me. Later on, the lessons of Big Rock would be part of the court file that would govern our lives for the next sixteen years.

As Nicholas grew, he came to realize that Big Rock is about twenty feet off the main trail and maybe all of two hundred yards from the parking lot. Of course, he also thought Big Rock had "shrunk." But it is still there, years later, unchanged — a solid testament to the way perceptions change with time.

It has been said that one's perception is one's reality. During my first week of law school, one of my adjunct professors, a practicing attorney and part-time teacher, expanded on that notion and shared a valuable and memorable lesson. She said, "The

THE FUTURE

If you want a new future, then you begin by creating a new history.

practice of law has nothing to do with the truth and everything to do with the perception of truth." This is reality — an only slightly exaggerated statement of fact that is perhaps most applicable when it comes to child custody litigation and all its twists, turns, and unhappy consequences.

In life in general or within the confines of a courtroom, those who think that they will prevail on the truth alone are often sourly disappointed. Sometimes such naivety results in people choosing to represent themselves in a divorce or child custody case. This is never advisable. If you are going though a separation, divorce, or child custody and visitation dispute you need good advice. When it comes to parenting effectively through a separation and divorce, if you do not get on the right path, you will likely, knowingly or otherwise, contribute to the ruination of your children. If things continue to spiral out of control, your children will be robbed of the innocence of childhood.

We will start our journey by addressing what is usually the most contentious area of parental discord: the children's residential and parental access schedule when their parents no longer live together. If it is possible to work out a schedule that is acceptable to both parents and beneficial to the children on many different levels, the rest of the needed changes and solutions to new problems are more likely to fall into place. However, it isn't easy and it requires much hard work and effort. You and you alone need to be the impetus for meaningful positive change.

When there is no governing court order or agreement in place, parental scheduling issues can be all consuming. There is often a heightened feeling of helplessness that exacerbates all related issues and concerns. In most cases, the worst time for custody chaos is shortly after the initial separation. The problems of the past are overshadowed by the current practical and emotional difficulties associated with adapting to dramatic and life-altering changes. The need for self-preservation and the protection of the well-being of one's children, along with huge financial adjustments, can be significant stressors.

During a breakup, emotions are high; feelings of anger, resentment, and other unpleasant emotions are thrown into the mix. A great uneasiness may loom about. The future is uncertain, and the "fear" (false evidence appearing real) — whether genuine, imagined, or exaggerated — can be overwhelming. There are often threats, tactical innuendoes, and power struggles whirling about. In the midst of such quagmires of turmoil there are impressionable children caught in the middle of ongoing child access disputes and doused in never-ending loyalty conflicts.

This book is designed to give you the suggestions, resources, and tools to bring stability, contentment, and, hopefully, some peace and happiness to your children. They are proven methods. The degree of their success depends first and foremost upon your willingness to change your behavior. That, in turn, will allow you to teach the other parent — by example. Except in the most extreme cases, avoid litigation at all costs. To be candid, complaints about personal injustice and wallowing in the "this isn't fair" chorus are of little concern to our family law court system. Judges are primarily concerned with the best interests of the children, not about you. What is truly in most children's best interests is to have two parents who can demonstrate by their words and actions that they love their children more than they dislike each other.

If there are regular and continued child-related arguments centered on phrases like the ones to follow, you just might be in for some tough times ahead.

- There is no "agreement" — so take it or leave it.
- It's not your scheduled time.
- They are planning on moving — what are my rights?
- I don't care if you made plans with our son, you shouldn't have.
- I'm not letting you have her until a judge tells me that I have to.
- I'm calling the police.
- I have to beg just to spend time with my child.
- Unless you sign this paper, or do this, or agree not to do that... you're not getting him.
- You can't tell me where to take my child or who she can be around.
- You were late bringing him to me; so I will be keeping him longer and to hell with your plans.
- What about a right of first refusal? You don't need a sitter; I am available and I want to spend the time with our children while you are out.
- I never get notified about school functions, report cards, or my child's medical appointments.
- No one ever returns my phone calls.
- He is always bad-mouthing me in front of the children.
- None of the things that I buy for my child ever get returned.
- I don't have the health insurance information.
- We disagree on the doctors and the way medical issues should be dealt with.
- No one provides me with anything!

☞ My vacation time was supposed to start this weekend and she won't let me take her.

☞ We have to take turns going on our son's field trips because we cannot get along well enough to ride on the same bus.

☞ We do not agree on our child's sports involvement or extracurricular activities.

☞ We don't agree on childcare providers.

☞ We have different views on education and religious upbringing.

☞ She ignores me.

☞ He tries to intimidate me.

☞ She is using our child as a weapon.

☞ He uses the children to spy on me.

☞ She tells the children to lie.

☞ His girlfriend keeps sticking her nose in our business.

☞ We don't agree about holidays.

☞ Why do I have to do all of the driving?

☞ Basically, we disagree about everything.

If any of these issues resonate with you, then you probably do not need to see illustrative case examples. You know what the problems look and feel like. Only a superior parent can do what needs to be done to bring about positive change in these situations. Will you rise to the challenges that lie ahead or will you surrender to a life of chaos for you and your children?

The truth is, it's easy for you, your ex, and your children to be miserable when you're dealing with the ongoing details of parenting with someone you no longer live with. It's not hard to unwittingly allow all of your anger and bad feelings to continue to disrupt your children's lives. There are a host of issues that nearly all separated and divorced parents deal with, and often they don't deal with them very well: transportation, school, extracurricular activities, medical issues, holidays and vacations, primary residence, child access and visitation issues, and keeping track of what's at mom's and what's at dad's. The devil is in the details, and it too often brings out the devil in us.

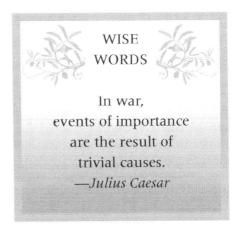

WISE WORDS

In war,
events of importance
are the result of
trivial causes.
—*Julius Caesar*

It doesn't have to. In this book we'll take a look at the everyday issues that prove troublesome for many separated and divorced parents, *with a special emphasis on the trials and tribulations of the recently separated.* We will explore ways to overcome the usual trouble spots. There is a way to preserve your children's innocence, to preserve your relationship with them, and even (or perhaps especially) to preserve your children's relationship with their other parent. It starts with developing the right mindset, attitude, and commitment to be the best parent that you can be — a superior parent.

Of course, everyone is busy these days — and no one is much busier than single parents. I know. That's why this book is written in relatively short, easy-to-read sections. You can read it through quite easily, or you can browse for the most applicable sections.

According to a survey of the nation's top divorce and family law lawyers conducted by the American Academy of Matrimonial Lawyers (AAML), the ten top mistakes that parents with children make during divorce are:

1. Denigrating the other spouse.
2. Using the child as a messenger.
3. Interfering with visitation rights.

4. Sharing intimate details of the other spouse's infidelity and behavior.
5. Failing to pay child support; inadequately supporting the children.
6. Immediately introducing the child to the parent's new love interest.
7. Moving the child as far away as possible from the other parent.

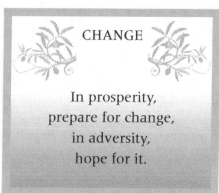

CHANGE

In prosperity,
prepare for change,
in adversity,
hope for it.

8. Listening to the child's conversations with the other parent.
9. Having the child read all of the legal pleadings or having them contact the attorney.
10. Having the child request money from the other parent.

You don't want to make these mistakes, or the many others that separated and divorced parents so frequently make. If you are going through a child custody battle, a child access or visitation dispute, or fear that you might, you could probably benefit from some sensible and affordable guidance. Even if you are far along in the process or living years later in the aftermath of divorce, you may occasionally encounter difficulties in dealing with your ex. The way you cope with the many situations arising from your separation and divorce will greatly determine how well your children cope. You are at a crossroads; take the high road, the path to Big Rock.

2

Splitting the Baby

When there is an ongoing fight over child access, it is important to realize that the term *stability,* in the context of fighting over the division of parental time, is an oxymoron if there is no agreed-upon schedule. For example, in some cases one parent may somewhat disingenuously stress that access to the other parent must be limited for the sake of the *stability* of the child. However, when there is an ongoing power struggle to maximize or minimize parental time, the life of the child is anything but "stable."

Children adapt. The world is busy. Life is hectic. The theories or justifications of years past, the "traditional visitation schedule" if you will, that subscribed to the notion that a child needs to only regard one parent's house as "home" and that he must sleep in the same bed every night is far less important than often proclaimed. These days, many experts suggest that a rigid "every other weekend and one or two nights a week for dinner" visitation schedule is a minimum type of arrangement. For separated or divorced parents, this is not necessarily the preferred norm.

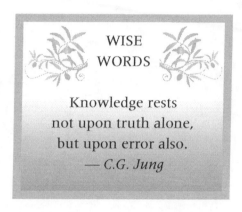

WISE WORDS

Knowledge rests not upon truth alone, but upon error also.
— *C.G. Jung*

Having parented for over a decade on a court-ordered, equal-time-sharing schedule, I can attest to the fact that even a nearly 50-50 type schedule is far more workable than one might imagine. While it is not presumed that 50-50 is best for all children in all situations, it sure seems like a fair place to start. Furthermore, I have found that if the parents truly opt to act in accordance with the children's best interests and if each parent operates from such a position of theoretical and practical equality, it is far more likely that one parent will voluntarily, if, when, and as needed, make the sacrifice of diminished time if it is truly beneficial to the *children's* schedule.

If dad, for example, has been treated as an equal parent and not a weekend visitor, there is a greater likelihood that he will go along with future modifications if the children's needs or routines suggest a modification to be appropriate. Once the power struggle for control and the claim for the overwhelming majority of time are abandoned, it simply will not be as important when compared to what may genuinely be in the children's best interests.

If the division of time is not mutually satisfactory, or if it is not otherwise possible to arrange a basic schedule with a certain amount of predictability (along with situational flexibility, respect, and cooperation), a court ordered schedule will ultimately be forced upon you. In such situations, any written document or court order must leave nothing open to interpretation. Your life must then fit into the court-mandated schedule. However, this is far easier and far less damaging to the children than the constant tug of war that often will occur in parental skirmishes. Simply left to the interpretation of loosely worded court orders, acrimonious parents will usually fail to rearrange or modify scheduled activities and time frames without wreaking havoc upon their children's lives. Let me show you how to minimize the problems that you may encounter.

REALITY CHECK

When parents are unable to work out the basic or primary residential schedule it is then necessary to have a rigid written schedule. A set schedule forces everyone — mom, dad, and children — to adjust their lives accordingly. The alternative to insufficient compromise is to surrender parental autonomy to the courts.

The Best Interest of the Child

When it comes to deciding cases involving children, the *best interest of the child standard* is the guiding principle. It has been said that the best interest standard really comes down to a judge's "best guess" as to what is optimal for a child in any particular case. And who is the judge and why is he or she the best person to make this decision for you and your children, well that's what this chapter is all about.

Parents in conflict will quickly learn the court lingo when it comes to child custody disputes. Everything that either party does is somehow, someway, supposedly linked to, and directly in pursuit of, what is in the "best interest" of the child or children at issue. The "ends justify the means" becomes the rationale for the parents in moderate- to high-conflict cases. High-conflict cases often result in false allegations and accusations. If the overall goal is to "win" custody, then does it matter if dad, for example, is falsely accused of inappropriate conduct with his child?

If mom is recklessly exaggerating or outright fabricating, as long as it is only in an effort to make dad "look bad" so that he will not likely get custody, is there any real harm done if that accomplishes what mom knows is

CHANGE

Change is not made without inconvenience, even from worse to better.
—*Richard Hooker*

really in her child's best interest? Probably not — at least not in the eyes of a selfishly blinded parent caught in a war of attrition. The sad reality is that in the majority of cases each parent tries to look his or her best by making the other parent look inept.

The run of the mill "we produced a child and now we hate each other" type of case is a mud-slinging contest with the echoing of the words, "in the best interest of the child." In the classic script of course, the man is always abusive, threatening, and intimidating and should only have supervised visitation to protect the safety of the child and the child's "best interests." The mother is referred to as slut and is accused of being inattentive to the physical or emotional needs of the child while also allegedly engaging in a scheme to alienate the child from the father and his whole side of the family. Furthermore, she is a liar, just ask anyone who knows her! Call your next witness.

The best interest of the child standard is not supposed to be a test on "good parent" vs. "bad parent" decision-making. However, although some state courts may characterize the criteria and terminology differently, the gist of the court's reasoning in deciding who gets the prize is to evaluate certain "factors." The court examines these factors and weighs the advantages and disadvantages of the alternative environments — who the children get to live with. The criteria for judicial determination include:

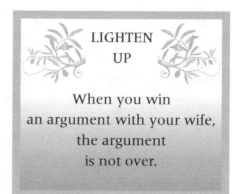

1. Fitness of the parents
2. Character and reputation of the parties
3. Desire of the natural parents and agreements between the parties
4. Potentiality of maintaining natural family relations
5. Preference of the children
6. Material opportunities affecting the future of the children
7. Age, health, and sex of the children
8. Residences of parents and opportunity for visitation
9. Length of separation from the natural parents
10. Prior voluntary abandonment or surrender of the child or children

At the conclusion of all the trial testimony, a judge, a complete stranger to you and your children, will say that he or she has examined the totality of the situation in light of these factors. He or she will say that the court has considered all the factors and that the decision was reached without specifically focusing on any one factor in and of itself. As far as all the lies that the court will have heard, expect that from the bench you will hear something like, "I have had an opportunity to observe the witnesses and assess their credibility and demeanor throughout these proceedings. And while I do have some credibility concerns, I believe that it is in little Johnny's best interest to remain in the care and custody of his mother."

When the best interest standard jargon is broken down, there are far more questions and concerns than there are answers and solutions. To illustrate, follow my logic as we examine just a couple of the ten aforementioned factors and weigh the advantages and disadvantages of each area of focus in relation to the other "facts" and factors.

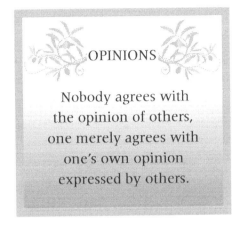

OPINIONS

Nobody agrees with the opinion of others, one merely agrees with one's own opinion expressed by others.

The court should consider the fitness of the parties. What in the hell does that mean? Let us say mom is physically fit and trim and dad is three hundred and fifty pounds and moves at a snail's pace, does that matter? What if mom is on antidepressant medication or in therapy? Who isn't in therapy of some sort these days? Many judges are not strangers to shrinks and such. But dad used to smoke pot and snort cocaine, how about that? Mom got a DUI charge last year on her birthday and the court made her go to a twenty-six-week alcohol program. Is she fit to have custody? Dad recently had a heart attack and mom has breast cancer, now what? Suppose that both have no such issues? Suppose they are equally fit or unfit?

While the financial fitness of the parties will likely be addressed too, in terms of material opportunities affecting the future of the children, where does it begin to significantly matter? The court will consider the character and reputation of the parties. Well, let's open the closet doors and let all the skeletons out! Ten years ago he hit his former girlfriend. She used to be a prostitute before going to college and earning her master's degree in early childhood development, now what? Dad had five witnesses say what a good person he is and one witness was a priest. Mom had six witnesses saying what a scoundrel dad has always been; and as for his priest witness, well eighteen years ago he allegedly molested mom's cousin. Dad once was convicted of petty theft, even though he contended that pulling out of the gas station without paying was an accident. It probably was, but nonetheless it is on his record. Oh, and let's not forget the smut sites he visits on the Internet and those chat rooms. He is such a womanizer! But

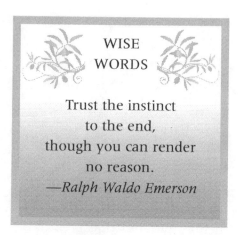

WISE WORDS

Trust the instinct
to the end,
though you can render
no reason.
—*Ralph Waldo Emerson*

what about those dirty pictures of her and his two best friends playing naked twister in a sleazy looking hotel room? What about the fact that he lied on his tax returns and makes twenty thousand dollars a year "under the table," does that matter? But she used the money for her and the kids and she signed the joint tax return too. Yes, but only because he forced her to do it and she had no choice; remember, he is abusive. All his ex-girlfriends hate him and all his family will lie for him. It goes on and on — all under oath to tell the truth, the whole truth, and nothing but the truth. The truth is that most parents will find little trouble telling a few lies if it will help them obtain custody of their children. How far would you go? How far would your ex go?

What is also interesting is that most of the terrible things the litigants say about each other were known before they ever had children together. When blinded by lust and maybe even love, these "minor" issues were overlooked. After all, no one is perfect and we have all done things that we are not proud of in life. During courtship, the same people may have said, "She's changed" or "You just have to really know him to understand."

Now, in litigation, the court is called upon to consider the desire of the natural parents and agreements between the parties.

Well, let's see. They are both fighting for custody of their child. They are willing to spend the equivalent of their child's college education on attorney's fees and litigation expenses. They will air out all their dirty laundry in public. Does the one who will stop at

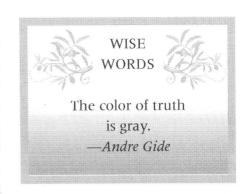

WISE WORDS

The color of truth is gray.
—*Andre Gide*

nothing to win have the most desire? Does he really want the children to live with him or is he is just trying to punish her for ending the relationship? Is it a little of both? Does it really matter what the motive is as long as the "best interests" of the children are served?

As far as the court considering past agreements between the parties, more "he said — she said." He claims he was promised 50-50 with the children until she found out that such an arrangement would significantly cut down on her monthly child support check. She claims that he only wanted to have them every other weekend at the most and he has never even changed a diaper.

The court might be asked to consider the preference of the child. This is a dangerous proposition and although courts may, depending on the age and maturity of the child, "consider" the preference of the child, the child's say is generally not much of a factor until approaching or into the teen years. Even then, it is one terrible place for a child to be. To ask a child to pick sides is downright cruel.

The court should also consider the potentiality of maintaining natural family relations. I firmly believe that this really should be a central focus of what it is all about, especially in high-conflict cases. Even if one parent seems significantly superior in general parenting skills yet constantly does all that is possible to restrict the children's access to the other parent, the resulting constant con-

flict and power struggle will
never be in the children's best
interests. One of the difficulties lies in proving the evil intent of the self-proclaimed
"superior parent" to under-
mine the importance of the
adverse or at-risk parent-child
relationship.

WARNING

Litigation is Harmful
to Your Children
— Proceed with Caution!

Again, litigants come to court armed with all the right things to
say. "He can see the children whenever he wants. I don't have a
problem with that. I want the children to have a great relationship
with their dad." Even if the trial judge is presented with examples
of mom restricting access or undermining the father's role, he or
she may simply attribute it to the temporary hostility of the court
proceedings and not recognize the deep-seated mindset that will
last throughout the child's minority years. The court is not going
to want to listen to all of the minor complaints of the parties and
usually only a small percentage of what each parent wants the court
to realize about his or her case is ever properly presented, if at all.
Furthermore, what may be of great importance to one or both of
the parties or to the lawyers may be of little, if any, significance to
the fact finder.

Hopefully, the judge will award primary custody to the parent
who will most allow the children to grow up with a mother and a
father actively involved in the children's lives. Often, that does not
happen and the children pay the price. If *you* do not settle your
child access issues following a separation or divorce, you will ultimately turn your children's fate over to a virtual stranger, a judge.

When it comes to following "the law," judges perhaps have the
most discretion in the area of child custody disputes. In practice,
they apply facts — or at least "facts" as they appear to them. They

decide what the facts are and they decide how to best remedy whatever facts they deem in need of judicial intervention. The "rules of law" give them great latitude when it comes to determining what they believe to be in a child's best interest. Ultimately, they make the major decisions per-

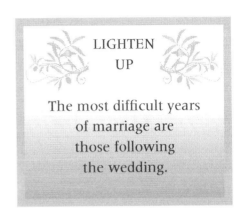

LIGHTEN UP

The most difficult years
of marriage are
those following
the wedding.

taining to each family law case. They, not you, get to decide how things will be. Such discretion may or may not be a good thing, depending on who is doing the judging and why.

Think about this. The judge comes on the bench and says that he has read the information in the case file and it looks like the same old nonsense that he sees day in and day out. He then goes into a stern lecture along the lines that he does not know your children, has never met them, and of all the people in the courtroom, he likely knows the least about them. Furthermore, even at the end of the case he will still know very little about your children. Yet, you two, the parents, are willing to let him, a complete stranger, tell you how you will raise your children.

"Make no mistake about it," the judge can rightly say, "I do have the complete and sole authority to order when each of you will see your child and when you will not. I can make the schedule for you. I can decide who makes all the decisions, some of the decisions, or none of the decisions. I can order you to all kinds of classes, treatment, and counseling if I find that there is a need and that it would be in your children's best interest. I will tell you when your vacation is and who will wake up with the children on Christmas morning. And when I am done, you are out of my thoughts and you will live with these rulings until your children reach the age of majority, or until you come back. When you come here to my courtroom, these children belong to me. I will hold onto this file. I'm the new daddy in town."

Certainly, by this time the parents are a nervous wreck. Something will sink into at least one of them. A good judge might continue, "You asked to be here and you still have a chance to get out. While you look like nice people, I don't know you and I really care very little about either of you. I do, fortunately, care a great deal about your children; apparently, I care more than each of you. I would never let a stranger decide the fate of my children. Now, I am going to go back into chambers and I want your lawyers to bring me as many resolved issues as possible and depending on your progress, I will decide when and how we proceed. I will be here until 5:00 p.m. and so will you, so I suggest you make the best of your day. It would be in your children's best interest for you to work all these issues out. Now, after all day, if you can't even decide on things like a holiday and vacation schedule, you surely are both going to leave here very unhappy. If we have to have a trial and if I have to make these decisions for you, I will have no qualms about any decision that I make. You may, but that is not my problem, it will be yours. Now, grow up, put your anger and pride aside, be parents. This is not a child friendly place. Now counsel, bring me an agreement on something within an hour. I know each of you highly skilled attorneys can work this out. Now, unless someone has something profound to say, we will remain in recess until you bring me an agreement on something. Have I made myself clear?"

More than likely you will be able to hear a pin drop amidst some sniffling from a teary-eyed mom or dad who may have had an awakening and be willing to negotiate in good faith. Hopefully, they will both be moved by such an "enlightening" monologue. Once the attorneys have their respective client's undivided attention, it is time to get to work. At some point in time there will be some agreement — even if the parties agree that on Mother's Day the children will be with their mother and on Father's Day they will be with their father. In building from there, they can further decide if these special days will be spent from say 10:00 a.m. until 8:00 p.m. or how about from the night before — Saturday night at 6:00 p.m. until Sunday at 6:00 p.m., for example? From there, perhaps a discussion and agreement on which parent shall provide the transportation on the Mother's Day and Father's Day exchanges would be appropriate. The lawyers can then build from there, and even the slow and tedious momentum of such "baby steps" on this path will be better than a leap of faith in a courtroom.

Even if the parents will never agree on who should have primary custody of their child, they can make two schedules, one if the children are with dad and one if they are with mom. Ideally, it may all be the same except for which parent will spend more time with the children. The judge can then simply decide, if still needed, which parent gets the better of the two agreed-upon schedules. Otherwise, the parties have no control over the ultimate outcome and it may be completely different than either of them expected.

Developing
a Schedule
4

T here are many ways to approach the development of a residential and access schedule. Rather than explain or justify any of them, let's start with a few basic principles.

- There is no *moral entitlement* to anything more than equally dividing the time the children spend with each parent.
- There is no *legal entitlement* to *equal* parenting time.
- If you and the other parent were both completely committed to working out a schedule that maximizes each parent's time with the children, you could do it.
- The children's best interests are usually served when measured within the reasonable and practical limits of life in general and balanced in particular with the parenting styles and attributes of each parent.

- If each parent felt secure that they would truly have reasonable and liberal time and access with their children, without being unreasonably rebuffed, the counting of overnights would become less important and a more *stable* schedule (whatever the percentage of time comes to be) would be more likely to develop on its own.
- The best schedule is one that minimizes conflict and maximizes the children's time with each parent.

Although maximizing parental time is very important, it should yield to the best interests of the children. And obviously, each parent's differing views about what is or is not in the children's best interests is one of the many contributors to child custody chaos. The desire for power and control are other major contributors, as you might expect.

Take Mandy and Randy for example. After eleven years of marriage, Randy rolled out with a younger model while his wife, Mandy, was still nursing their three-month-old baby girl. Their older daughter was four years old. Randy took up residence with a separated co-worker and her six-year-old son about sixty-five miles away from the former marital home. After some short-lived talks of reconciliation, the parties came to the realization that their marriage was over; it got ugly for a while. To Mandy's credit, she did not seek to punish Randy by using the children as bargaining chips. She knew then that it was important for their daughters to have a positive relationship with their father, regardless of the way he had betrayed her.

Mandy offered for Randy to spend more time with the girls than he actually utilized, but they could not agree to an overnight schedule as Randy would not move from his 50-50 position. Often, if he could not *have* his daughters overnight, because Mandy would not agree to it during the work week, Randy *chose not* to see his daugh-

ters. What he failed to acknowledge was that given the
distance between the two
homes (which he also chose),
he would have to wake the
girls at the crack of dawn to
get them to daycare before
clocking in at the factory at
7:00 A.M. Such a schedule
wasn't workable. When the
girls were with their mother,
they slept until 7:00 A.M. Sim-

JUDGMENT

Good judgment
comes from experience,
and experience,
well, that comes from
bad judgment.
Be the superior parent.

ilarly, the fact that the baby suffered severe separation anxiety from
her mother was of no concern to Randy. To this selfish dad, he was
their father and he demanded his "50 percent inalienable rights"
as he called them. The impracticalities of the situation, to him, were
irrelevant.

Mandy proposed that Randy see the children whenever he wanted during the week as long as they were back to their mother by
8:00 P.M. Reasonable notice for this would be expected. On the
weekends, she was fine with them spending every other weekend
from Friday until Sunday night with their father. Dividing holidays
and allocating vacation was not problematic for Mandy. Randy
could not fathom that a judge would have a problem with disrupting the children's routines on weekdays so that he got his 50
percent time with his daughters. Oh, did I mention that reducing
his child support obligation was a driving factor in all of his settlement negotiations?

Poor Randy, his proclaimed 50 percent inalienable parental
rights gave way to reason and logic. The judge agreed with Mom.

When trying to work out a schedule, remember that compromise
is far more than counting days and overnights. The practicalities of

travel time, distance, parental work schedules, daycare, school, friends, and extracurricular activities all need to be taken into consideration, with the best interests of the children of paramount concern.

Litigants must realize that the courts cannot really mandate behavior. The courts can only provide a framework from which to live. (For sample language and clauses to incorporate into your parenting and access schedules, and parenting agreements, see appendices A, C, and D.)

> WISE WORDS
>
> The man who grasps principles can successfully select his own methods. The man who tries methods, ignoring principles, is sure to have trouble.
> —*Ralph Waldo Emerson*

People who think the courts will *solve* their parental disputes are sadly mistaken. The quality of life that parents offer to their children is up to them. The sooner we realize this, the better off everyone will be.

Litigation, "Winning," and the Status Quo

5

I n child custody litigation, it is no secret that when a case comes to court, the judges are reluctant to change the status quo if things are generally working out for the children. This concept of maintaining the status quo is similar in theory to not rocking the boat, upsetting the apple cart, or trying to fix what isn't broken. It is a simple concept that can cause huge problems when two stubborn parents are preparing for court and jockeying for position to be awarded primary custody. What follows is an example of how some "traditional" legal advice only fosters acrimonious litigation. All too often the perpetual fighting starts when parents ask the wrong questions and the lawyers provide some accurate, but "wrong" answers.

Let's start with a hypothetical scenario, which is commonly seen in real life. The parents do not belong together and everyone knows it. Their child is of tender years. There is no reason why either parent would not be able to raise the child on his or her own and adequately care and provide for the youngster. Neither individual is a "bad" person. They are both employed. Together they are like fire and gasoline. Both are intelligent and both have had experience with lawyers and litigation in their respective personal and professional lives. Regardless of their stated

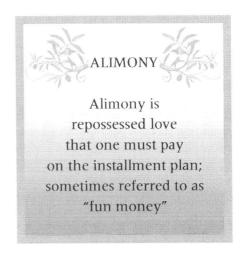

ALIMONY

Alimony is
repossessed love
that one must pay
on the installment plan;
sometimes referred to as
"fun money"

reasons for wanting to have sole legal and physical custody of their child, they are in a struggle for control of the situation.

Mom seeks a top-notch big law firm lawyer who she knows and trusts and the following occurs:

Mrs. Client: "Jeff, tell me, how do I make sure that he does not get custody of Joey? I want custody and I don't know what visitation he should get. My husband said that he wants Joey to live with him and for me to have visitation. He said he will fight for full custody if I do not agree to a 50-50 schedule. He is the one that moved out. How often should I let him see Joey? And, what about child support, how much can I get?"

Mr. Lawyer: "Connie, the way for you to win and to optimize your child support is simple. You should only let him have Joey every other weekend from Friday until Sunday and one night a week. These cases take so long to come to trial that by the time it comes to court, if your husband has only had Joey every other weekend and one overnight during the week, it will most likely not change. You two can share or divide the holidays and each of you could get a week or two of summer vacation and things like that. If he has your son more than 128 overnights out of a year, under our state's child support guidelines, he may be able to pay you less child support than if he were to have Joey on a more limited basis. So, you need to control the schedule."

Mrs. Client: "But what about now? He keeps pressing me to let him have *my son* half of the time and he said that if I keep refusing to agree to 50-50 he will hire a lawyer to file for an emergency hearing."

Mr. Lawyer: "Well, since he moved out and given the fact that your house is the child's primary residence, your husband has an uphill battle. You need to call the shots. We can propose different schedules and appear to be flexible, but we just need to limit his overnights so as to maintain the status quo in your favor. As far as emergencies go, in the eyes of the court, unless there is blood and guts or someone is going to take the child out of the country forever, there are not many things that are considered *emergencies*."

Mrs. Client: "Yeah, but he keeps calling, e-mailing, and faxing me letters that say I am not letting him see his son and that I promised 50-50 before he moved out, so what do I do?"

Mr. Lawyer: "Well, you should really limit the contact and communication. If you feel as if he is just badgering you, we could insist that all communication will have to go through the lawyers. Just basically ignore him; but you can't completely deny visitation. As long as you are offering something along the lines of what I suggested, your husband will not be able to get any emergency hearing or anything like that."

Mrs. Client: "Thanks so much, Jeff. I feel so much better!"

Of course, the calculating husband has consulted with his lawyer and his lawyer told him that Connie would likely do all of the above. How does he know that? Well, if Connie came to him with the goal of "winning" primary custody and maximizing her child support, he, like any "decent" lawyer, would have basically advised the same.

The husband's attorney has advised his client to keep asking for the child and to document every request and every response or lack of response. He was instructed to keep a diary, journal, and a calendar of significant events and parental interaction with the goal to have as close to fifteen overnights per month as possible. Now that these two already headstrong people know the rules of engagement, so to speak, all hell is set to break loose; and in such a scenario, it will.

The way to avoid disaster and best provide for your children is to start asking the right questions:

- ☞ What does winning really mean in these cases?
- ☞ How can I avoid a custody battle?
- ☞ What is fair?
- ☞ In general, what is the best schedule for children of separation and divorce?
- ☞ What would work best for *our* children?
- ☞ How can we avoid damaging our children?
- ☞ How can we reduce the costs of the divorce?
- ☞ How can we reduce the anger and hostility?
- ☞ How can we learn to get along better, at least when it comes to our children?
- ☞ How can we learn to be flexible, so that things adjust as our children's needs change?

REALITY CHECK

By not fighting to maintain a status quo for the wrong reasons, you can actually build a more dignified and productive status quo by asking the right questions and seeking the right answers. But first, you must lose the anger and avoid contributing to any residual hostilities directed at you.

Here are some of the right answers:

- ☞ You "win" a child custody battle by avoiding one.
- ☞ You avoid a child custody battle by being fair and reasonable.
- ☞ Being fair means being respectful of your children's relationship with the other parent.
- ☞ The best schedule for children is one that optimizes the amount of time and involvement that both parents have.

The best schedule considers the needs of the children as well as the practicalities of everyone's schedule.

☞ Avoid damaging your children by showing that each parent loves them unconditionally.

☞ Encourage your children to spend time with, and love, both parents.

☞ Reduce the costs by reducing the anger and hostility and by being fair and reasonable.

☞ Reduce the anger and hostility by being fair, reasonable, and cordial.

☞ Seek counseling if you are having difficulty coping.

☞ Take advantage of the many resources, books, tapes, and educational materials that can help you learn to communicate more effectively.

☞ Become a student of positive parenting.

☞ Work on self-improvement and be the best parent that you can be.

Custody & Visitation: Parent-Friendly Terms? 6

W hen it comes to establishing each parent's individual roles and their levels of involvement, influence, and time spent with the children, the terms most discussed and debated are *joint custody*, *sole custody*, and *visitation*. Generally, physical child custody (whether sole, shared, or split) really comes down to the amount of time spent with one's children. Custody in the legal sense (that is, legal custody) governs who will make what types of decisions affecting the health, education, and general welfare of the children and under what circumstances such decisions will be made.

Basically, without further definition or limitation, a parent with sole legal custody calls all the significant shots with or without the other parent's "consent" or input. The term *custody* is anything but child friendly and its usage often provokes anger and resentment between bickering parents. The word *custody* in its basic and primary sense suggests possession and control. Police take "custody" of criminals. Enough said.

In moderate to highly contentious cases, the initial fight for control is often a key catalyst to a perpetual battle. The children's feelings and emotional well-being often get lost in all the posturing that accompanies one's desire to show the other parent who is in the driver's seat. This fighting over the children can resemble a game of capture-the-flag, where children are treated like possessions and rewards for success in battle.

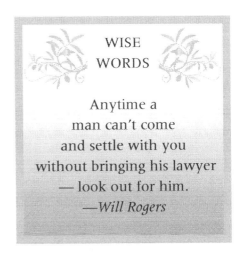

WISE WORDS

Anytime a man can't come and settle with you without bringing his lawyer — look out for him.
—Will Rogers

The counterpart to custody is visitation. What does the term *visitation* suggest? I "visit" clients in jail. Priests "visit" the dying in hospitals and nursing homes. Doesn't "visitation" suggest a short stay? Perhaps like a trip to a distant relative's house? Generally, we visit people or places that we don't see too often. When we are young we shouldn't be "visiting" our parents, we should be spending time with them. A parent's perception of terms like *custody* and *visitation* often fosters power-based and position-oriented discussions. This is usually not productive when the lives of our children are at stake.

In recognizing the power of suggestion and influence that can be derived from legal terms and principles in the area of family law, legal wizards have made significant efforts in the last decade or so to use more appropriate terms when discussing how to govern the lives of our children and the parent-child relationships that are affected by separation and divorce. These days, custody and visitation are more appropriately discussed in terms of *child access* and *parental involvement.* Legal custody is couched in terms of *parental decision-making.* Custody orders are referred to as *residential schedules.* Plaintiffs and Defendants are addressed as "Mother" or "Father"; and it is common for "the minor child of the parties" to be called by his or her name in legal documents. These are positive and long overdue steps in the right direction.

> **REALITY CHECK**
>
> The end of the relationship does not mean the end of the parental relationship. An unworkable marriage does not necessarily result in an unworkable parenting relationship.

Parents who are caught up in "child access disputes" should take special care to focus their respective and combined efforts in arriving at a fair and reasonable "parenting plan" and a "residential schedule" that works best for their children. An agreement should promote peace and stability between the parents as well. It is a lot easier to make positive progress and ensure meaningful child access and involvement when moms and dads use "parent-friendly" language in discussions about "custody" and "visitation."

7 Getting Your Emotions In Check

Separation, divorce, and child custody battles are "mind fields" of stress and anxiety. Prolonged and unnecessary fighting may affect your overall quality of life more than you realize. It can be overwhelming. Worse yet, it all trickles down to your children, especially during the crazy times.

It has been said that fear is the mother of all emotions. The fight or flight syndrome is simply a part of humanity that dates back to caveman days, an animal-like response that drives our behavior in times of perceived vulnerability. Life during an acrimonious child custody battle produces the same chronic heightened state of alertness, helplessness, and fear of the unknown. The feelings are just as real as those experienced in immediate life-threatening situations. Without going into a science lesson or mental health dissertation, suffice it to say that stress, fear, and anxiety are more than just unpleasant experiences. These feelings can and do cause physical and mental problems. No one is immune. When entrenched in parental warfare, you are physically and mentally at your worst. It affects your quality of life and the lives of everyone around you, especially your children.

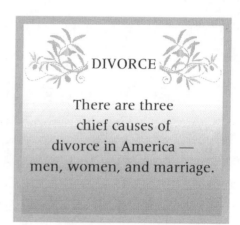

DIVORCE

There are three chief causes of divorce in America — men, women, and marriage.

Be aware that:

- ☞ The mind is a powerful weapon, and it can lead us to self-destruction.
- ☞ The mind's effects on the body can take its toll without our conscious awareness.
- ☞ Long-term aggravation, with no end in sight, is unhealthy.
- ☞ Prolonged stress, the constant up and down feelings, the false alarms, and the recurring "what's next?" thoughts can lead to dramatic and uncontrollable physical and psychological consequences.
- ☞ A custody battle is unpredictable.

Remember:

- ☞ Physical fitness and exercise help keep the mind strong too. Get off the couch, go out, do things.
- ☞ Try to compartmentalize your life in certain areas by designating certain days or times to work on your divorce, separation, or child-related issues. At other times, try to just get on with life. Things still need to get done at home and at work.

- Don't constantly talk about your family problems to non-professionals.
- If you talk about it all the time, even your friends and loved ones will eventually distance themselves. Everyone has problems, and there is little they can do anyway.
- Consider groups like Parents Without Partners, Divorce Care, or other support groups. Learn from people who genuinely understand what you are going through.
- Internet dating and "pen pals" might be a good outlet, but be careful about your e-mail being subject to hacking or subpoena.
- Counseling or therapy can help anyone, including you. It is not just for "sissies" or the "weak."
- Don't be afraid of being negatively stigmatized by therapy or prescription medication. Judges understand the pressures and they usually want to help people who recognize they need assistance and who are committed to self-improvement.
- When your children are with you, spend that time interacting with them.
- If you're having trouble sleeping, talk to your doctor. Sleep deprivation can greatly contribute to chronic depression.
- Do not use your children as your emotional crutch. Try not to let them know how upset and scared you are; but do always reassure them that you love them unconditionally.
- Drugs and alcohol are temporary panaceas that further complicate matters. Don't excessively drink alcohol; don't do drugs.
- Look for ways to laugh.
- Limit the size of "to do" lists.
- Prioritize more and focus on the most important things in your life more than ever.

➢ Now would be a good time to focus on getting organized.

Getting Your Life Organized

When we talk about enhancing the capacity to prevent and resolve conflict, we need to include organizational skills in the conversation. Personally speaking, I learned about the importance of being organized in the midst of chaos. I learned this out of necessity, not out of curiosity or from following good habits. During

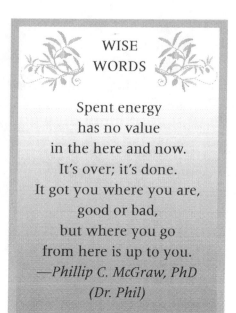

WISE WORDS

Spent energy
has no value
in the here and now.
It's over; it's done.
It got you where you are,
good or bad,
but where you go
from here is up to you.
—*Phillip C. McGraw, PhD*
(Dr. Phil)

times of significant transition, much of our personal and professional organizational capacity drops markedly. This in turn, decreases productivity, making it tougher to manage normal demands, not to mention the added ones that accompany parenting through separation and divorce.

During times of child custody chaos, your life may seem anything but organized. And, unfortunately, there is a vicious cycle involving the lack of organization and stress. Personally, the more disorganized I become, the more stressed I feel. When we are stressed out, it is also harder to stay organized. So, a chaotic cycle sets in. Can you relate? The issues of separation and divorce often present an organizational crisis. At the same time, they provide a prime opportunity for getting organized.

For a couple facing separation, for starters, there is the realization that it often takes the financial teamwork of *two* to sustain *one* household. Now there will be two separate homes and less "togetherness." People still need to work, manage the mail, pay the bills, cart the children here and there, and juggle all sorts of routine demands of time and energy. There are countless added emotional and financial commitments associated with the reconfiguring of the family. All of this takes time — a lot of time. You no longer can afford to waste time looking for things and reinventing the wheel.

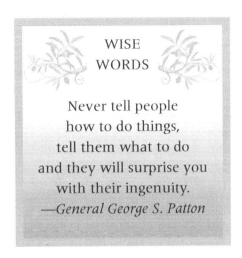

WISE WORDS

Never tell people how to do things, tell them what to do and they will surprise you with their ingenuity.
—*General George S. Patton*

For most people, getting organized is a worthy objective that tends to get "back burnered." During these chaotic times, you may occasionally have a heightened dose of energy and getting organized can become an exercise of productivity. Harness and direct some of that negative energy into something that can save you an abundance of time and aggravation in the years ahead. You can find some great organizational resources online.

Dispute-resolution experts spend a lot of time talking about how important it is for parties to learn how to think outside the box. However, it is difficult to do without first having a box and knowing what is in it. So, for many clients, the starting point is getting organized enough to know what you are facing by doing a reality check. Making it a priority to organize your life will ease the transition and help you sustain higher levels of productivity and enjoyment over the long term.

Turning the Corner

One of the hardest things to realize, while in the thick of it all, is that life will get better. Trust me. It will. Personally, it used to really tick me off when people would say things like, "Don't worry, it will all work out" or "Things will get better soon." It just doesn't sound or feel true when feelings of despair and self-pity are overwhelming you. It's possible to get stuck in a downward spiral of hopelessness. I did. Your fi-

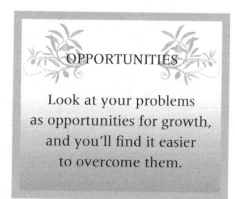

OPPORTUNITIES

Look at your problems as opportunities for growth, and you'll find it easier to overcome them.

nancial resources steadily dwindle. You become unproductive at work. You can't sleep. You throw up. You can't eat. You have no energy or motivation. You have difficulty focusing, and you have that zombie look about you. And all while your children need you the most.

However, the first step to healing is to "turn the corner." Accept the fact that there is no reconciliation on the horizon, no getting back together. Make it *your choice* (even if it was not at the outset) to put the past relationship behind you. Turn the corner and get on with your business — the business of parenting.

I promise you that at this precise moment next year, your life will be better or worse than it is right now. It will not be the same; the choice to improve it or let it decay is wholly and undeniably yours.

8

Why Forgiveness Matters

Many people believe that the opposite of love is hate. Not true. The opposite of love is *indifference*, especially in the context of a bitter separation or divorce. If the thought of the other parent and all of the mean and nasty things that they have done to you or against you interferes with the way that the two of you raise your children, you need to lose the anger, or at least regroup and channel it proactively. By turning those feelings of loathing into feelings of indifference, you can rid yourself of a great deal of emotional wear and tear.

Life is too short to go around full of bitterness. Childhoods are shorter. Before you know it, children will be adults. When children mature and later understand how they were "used" by one parent against the other out of anger (and they do figure it out), they will likely resent at least one of their parents, if not both. When there is the temptation to put the children in the middle of adult conflicts, you must always re-member that the true best in-terests of the children are served when there is genuine child-focused decision-mak-ing. Anger often gets in the way of that.

LOVE & HATE

People hate as they love, unreasonably
—*Thackeray*

It has been said that anger is often related to a real or perceived need to stand up for your worth, your needs, and your deepest sense of conviction. It may also stem from a sense of re-jection. In fact, anger is a label we give to a very hurtful emotion-al response. In divorce, more often than not, your sense of worth takes a beating. The reasons why you are angry and how you are conveying your feelings of anger are really important. Your qual-ity of life is not good when you cling to anger. Even though ex-pressing your emotions in the form of anger may feel good at the moment, it usually just makes things worse in the long run. Be-sides, parenting is hard enough without anger clouding your judg-ment and exhausting your patience.

Often the desire to be "in control" can be motivated by anger. Worse yet, the value system of the other person may be way out of balance from what you believe, thus setting the stage for dis-putes to take on a life of their own. Your former partner may say or do things that make you constantly feel like you have to respond in kind (and I am not talking about responding with kindness), thus fanning the flames and keeping the fight cycle in high gear.

When we feel extremely pressured or too controlled, our nat-ural desire is to want to recapture control. Therefore, it's easy to see how divorce can lead to a long-term power struggle. This very naturally pulls you into an awful lot of frustrating circumstances; the net result is a compounding of anger. Prolonged anger will eat you alive from the inside out. Misery can become the norm. When children are involved, it is a recipe for chaos.

To improve our situation we need to understand that there are reasons for the way things are and we need to be able to recognize our con-

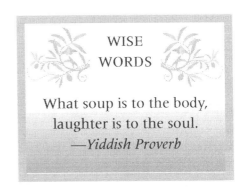

WISE WORDS

What soup is to the body, laughter is to the soul.
—*Yiddish Proverb*

tributing factors. Not until we first recognize and acknowledge *our* contributions to the cycle of dysfunction will we be able to discover and actively implement ways to change things for the better. Inappropriately dealing with our feelings often fuels our anger.

Here are a dozen helpful tips to avoid adult temper tantrums:

1. Healthy food habits and lifestyle choices are important.
2. Crying can sometimes be helpful. Think of it as a cleansing.
3. Stop the anger triggering "self-talk."
4. Exercise regularly, perhaps try yoga for body-mind balance and have regular intense workouts.
5. Humor and laughter are very healthy mood adjusters; maybe go to a comedy club.
6. Writing about your situation can help you focus.
7. Relaxation exercises can help.
8. Talk about your feelings, but do so with caution. Perhaps seek professional guidance from a counselor or spiritual advisor.
9. Recreation is a good thing. Get involved in enjoyable activities. Find new hobbies.
10. Sex can be a good stress reducer (even going solo can help).
11. Music can be very soothing.
12. Take time to rest or simply "chill."

The truth is, you may never *feel* ready to forgive your ex; it's simply up to you to decide it's time to do so. Being angry hurts you, not the other person. When you forgive, you free yourself. Go to the other person and seek forgiveness for the things you have done wrong in expressing your anger. Often just the simple

FORGIVENESS

Always forgive
your enemies —
nothing annoys them
so much.
—*Oscar Wilde*

acknowledgement that you have done wrong is all that is needed.

Deep anger can get in the way of our spiritual lives. We need to move beyond our anger to a better place within. Until you get there, at least learn to be indifferent. Without forgiveness you are destined to a life marred by anger, bitterness, and hatred.

Another really key concept to embrace is that assertive anger can be put to good use. Anger is usually accompanied by a component of energy, albeit often negative. However, those negative forces can be harnessed and channeled into great motivators. Get motivated to become a superior parent.

9 Transitions

W hen things are ugly (and sometimes even when they're not), one of the most difficult times for separated or divorced parents is when the children are going from one parent to the other and both parents are present at the "exchange." Generally, this time frame is referred to as "transition time." Even in the best of circumstances it is a stressful time for the children. Nothing gives children the feeling that they are caught in the middle quite like the transition.

Often, transition time is a sad reminder for the children that they are frequently placed in "no-win" situations. Even the youngest of children easily picks up on the tension. When there are arguments, threats, insults, stonewalling tactics, or silent treatments and general rudeness, what are the children thinking and absorbing? Surprisingly, some parents are oblivious to what is going on.

A Transition Blunder

Lynn and Steve's separation was anything but amicable. They argued and fought constantly, often directly in front of the children. Things were so bad that their attorneys made arrangements for the transitions to occur at the local police station. The thinking behind this was that the likelihood for the parties to act up, or for things to escalate, would be minimized. Not so.

The transition rendezvous had been set for 5:00 p.m. in the police department parking lot. When Steve arrived with the seven- and nine-year-old children, all hell broke loose when Lynn observed their youngest child stuffing her face with the last bites of a cheeseburger, while the eldest child was wiping chocolate ice cream from his face. Lynn was furious.

REALITY CHECK

By minimizing the anger that we "cause" the other parent, we help ourselves. You need to lead the other parent off the anger path. When the other parent realizes that they no longer can get to you by doing what used to always provoke you, the behavior will stop. It will no longer be "rewarding."

Before the children even exited their father's vehicle, Lynn bellowed, "Why are they eating? You know that I feed them at six o'clock, and dinner is already prepared!"

"Why are they eating?! Because they were freakin' hungry, you stupid bitch!"

"Don't you threaten me! HELP!" shouted Lynn.

A few minutes later a police officer walked over and intervened.

Steve continued, "You can't cook anyway! You are lucky that I even brought them back!"

Transitioning at the police station sends terrible messages to the children and usually does not act as much of a deterrent for parents who behave badly in front of their children. Obviously, Steve and Lynn's conduct is not exemplary. If you're having trouble envisioning a smooth transition from your house to your ex's, consider these dos and don'ts.

WISE WORDS

If you are patient
in one moment of anger,
you will escape
a hundred years
of sorrow.
—*Chinese epigram*

Transition Dos

☞ Be cordial. The best way to handle bad situations related to the exchange of the children is simply to be cordial. Say hello and good-bye. If you're dropping off the children, say, "Have fun" or "See you later." *Show your children that it is simply right to be polite.*

☞ Always be on time.

☞ Get your hugs and kisses prior to the exchange.

☞ Be mindful of your body language and demeanor.

☞ If it's Mother's Day, Father's Day, or some meaningful holiday, help the children pick out an appropriate gift or card to take to the other parent.

☞ Do your best not to show that you are uncomfortable in the presence of the other parent.

☞ Minimize the amount of stuff (toys, clothes, books, and so forth) that goes from house to house.

☞ Break the cycle of negative communication and dysfunction.

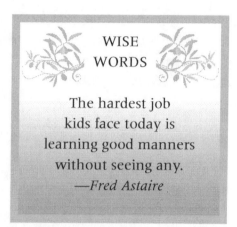

WISE WORDS

The hardest job kids face today is learning good manners without seeing any.
—*Fred Astaire*

⌐ Demonstrate that you are the superior parent at all times and in all situations.

Transition Don'ts

⌐ Don't "discuss" *anything*, especially early on in the process. Other than immediate health concerns, like, "You might want to have a doctor look at that gash in Timmy's head and here is a towel to stop the bleeding until you get him to the hospital," nothing else needs to be discussed *then and there*, at transition time. Nothing.

⌐ In case that wasn't clear, let me repeat myself. Don't discuss *anything*. Do not even think about having a discussion about money or child support at transition time. Do not make criticisms, suggestions, sarcastic comments (one of my personal favorites), ultimatums, or requests for anything, such as additional time with the children or changes in plans or scheduling. All of this will probably end in an argument or dirty looks or some other counterproductive exchange if there is any parental tension looming about.

⌐ Do not dwell on good-byes with the children. They will be just fine.

⌐ Do not tell your children to relay messages or information.

⌐ Do not give dirty looks or roll your eyes.

⌐ Do not say or do anything that would likely make the other parent uncomfortable — avoid hot buttons!

⌐ Do not bring your new girlfriend or boyfriend — they have no business being involved in the exchange.

- Do not pawn off the responsibility for transition. Show your children that you are either excited about their return or care enough to be there to say, "See you later."
- Do not allow yourself to get drawn in to nonproductive interaction.

REALITY CHECK

Transitions provide good practice to minimize the uncomfortable feelings for other times when you and the other parent will have to be together in the presence of the children for longer periods of time — such as graduations, awards ceremonies, sporting events, weddings, and funerals.

Take the Lead

Transitions are an opportunity to demonstrate to your children that they don't have to fear the rare times you and your ex are together. While you are probably capable of exercising great restraint from provocation, you may generally be worried about that idiot who just has to start with you at every opportunity. I understand. I have been the cordial one and I have also been the idiot. You will likely make mistakes at transition times too. It is not easy to keep your cool amid unpleasant changes. Recognize your errors and work to improve the situation. It takes time, but the sooner the better. The professionals will tell you the obvious: only you can control your behavior. This may be true, but your actions and reactions can help set the stage to hedge the odds in favor of "normal" human interaction in the future. As we tell our children, be leaders, not followers.

You're Late!

Y ou might think that "lateness" would be a trivial issue compared to the many more substantive concerns associated with child access disputes. Invariably though, the complaint of lateness, especially at transition time, is a hot spot between parents in conflict. It is also one of the more frequent complaints that divorce attorneys hear from their clients. Allowing yourself to disrupt your time with your child because you are bent out of shape over the other parent's tardiness is generally a non-productive expenditure of your time and energy. Let's look at a real-life example.

Carl was a typical angry parent. His wife had left him. There was an affair on her part and she claimed years of verbal abuse and denigration by Carl. The three children were very much aligned with their mother. Visitation was minimal and there was a temporary order regarding the pick-up and drop-off of the minor children. In this case rather than have Carl come to her house to pick up the children, Donna consented to doing all the driving.

Donna was to have the children to their father by 5:30 p.m. To Carl, 5:30 p.m. meant 5:30 p.m., not 5:35, and certainly not 6:00 p.m.! Donna got off work at 5:00 p.m. as she always had

LATE

Better late
than never,
but better never late.

throughout the marriage. Now, post-separation, she would have to drive a little further to get home to her new apartment, round up the children, and head back out into the rush-hour traffic. Whenever they arrived at the former family home, typically about ten to twenty minutes late, Carl would be pacing on the porch. When Donna's vehicle headed up the driveway, he would walk to the vehicle while pointing at his watch. The ranting and raving would usually end with an exchange of insults. Of course, all of this took place in front of the children.

Typically, the first half hour or so of the transition time would be tense and unpleasant for everyone. Carl would grill the kids about why their mother was late and what time they left. Often, this conversation would flow into bad-mouthing the children's mother. And, when it was time for the children to be picked up, things would tense up all over again. Carl would tell the children that it was time to pack up and then follow up with a comment like, "Well, why bother, she is always late anyway." Occasionally, he would add a comment or two suggesting that Donna was probably out "whoring around."

Donna would usually arrive a few minutes late on the pick-up as well. In fact, Donna had never been a punctual person. Carl had accepted this throughout their marriage, but not now! When the children went back with their mom, she would ask them how Carl acted when they went into the house. Now it was her turn to do the bad-mouthing! The children would then be asked to "tell on dad" just like dad had required them to "tell on mom" when they arrived. Needless to say, the children never looked forward to their transitions.

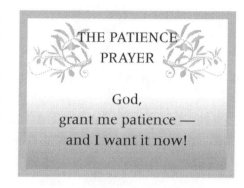

THE PATIENCE PRAYER

God,
grant me patience —
and I want it now!

Since Carl was my client, I had the duty and responsibility to help him put things in proper perspective. My advice consisted of the same discourse that I have been giving parents for many years. In short, if you're complaining about lateness, you probably need to focus on something else.

Here's what I told Carl:

- ☞ Be grateful that you are getting to see your children; it could be worse.
- ☞ Waiting at your home is far better than waiting on the other parent's front porch.
- ☞ If she is "always" fifteen to twenty minutes late and she is supposed to arrive at 5:30, pretend that she is supposed to arrive by 6:00 p.m. Then, when she and the children arrive at 5:50 p.m., you can "rejoice" that they are ten minutes early.
- ☞ By complaining about it, the other parent knows that it gets to you; don't give her the satisfaction.
- ☞ Think about how your actions are diminishing the quality of the time that you *do* get to spend with your children.
- ☞ You should make your children feel like you are overjoyed to see them, not bummed out at the time of their arrival.

☞ As far as the courts are concerned, generally people who complain about a few minutes here and there, or an occasional substantial deviation from punctuality, look like idiots when they waste time squabbling over such things. There are more important issues to be concerned about.

☞ When you are supposed to have the children some place at a particular time — just do it.

☞ Teach by example.

☞ Things don't always work out just right; people will be late from time to time.

☞ Shit happens.

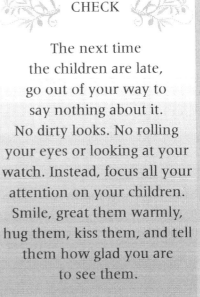

REALITY CHECK

The next time the children are late, go out of your way to say nothing about it. No dirty looks. No rolling your eyes or looking at your watch. Instead, focus all your attention on your children. Smile, great them warmly, hug them, kiss them, and tell them how glad you are to see them.

The world is a busy place and the twenty-first century is replete with more and more things to do. The same technological revolution that is supposed to make our lives simpler and more convenient often interferes with our parenting time. How many times do cell phones, e-mails and video games get in the way of the limited amount of actual parenting time that is available? Sometimes it is necessary to slow down in order to make progress in your parenting practices.

11

Communication

Whr it comes to conflict between separated and divorced parents, poor communication is usually at the heart of the problem. If you didn't communicate well when you were together, the chances of doing so now are slim. Uncertainty and its accompanying fears and concerns, especially pertaining to the well-being of the children, make positive interaction all the more difficult. For the two of you to develop good communication skills now may seem like an insurmountable obstacle, but I've seen people do it.

Perhaps one of the best things you can do to improve the quality of life for your children is to improve your listening skills and interpersonal communication techniques so that you can more effectively interact with the other parent. Of course, it's true that you can only control your behavior and your former spouse may have no interest in improving his or her communication skills. But, the truth is that the more controlled *you* are, the better the chances are that the other parent may one day just learn to do the same. Remember "monkey see, monkey do"?

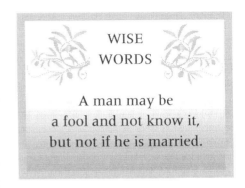

WISE WORDS

A man may be a fool and not know it, but not if he is married.

One helpful communication tool is "I messages." I recommend learning how to use them. What is an "I message?" An "I message" is a distinct communication technique with four essential parts:

1. Identifying the problem.
2. Stating how you feel.
3. Stating why you feel that way.
4. Making a specific request for change.

A simple example of an "I message" may sound like this: "When you are late dropping off Sally at my house on Wednesday evenings, it makes it difficult for me to get her to bed on time. The next morning she is tired and cranky. This is very frustrating to me and not good for her. I would greatly appreciate it if you return her to me on time from now on."

By voicing your concerns through use of the "I message," you avoid criticizing the other parent and give them the request for positive action. For some additional information on "I messages" and parental communication in general, I highly recommend reading *Joint Custody with a Jerk, Raising a Child with an Uncooperative Ex*, by Julie A. Ross, M.A., Director of Parenting Horizons, and Judy Cocoran. *Joint Custody with a Jerk* is a hands-on, practical guide to coping with custody issues that arise with an uncooperative ex-spouse.

There are many sources of instruction and guidance in the area of communication skills. Here is a short version of guidelines that many parents have found helpful in resolving conflict and helping to communicate more effectively with the other parent.

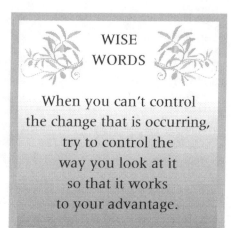

WISE WORDS

When you can't control the change that is occurring, try to control the way you look at it so that it works to your advantage.

Communication Dos

- ☞ Voluntarily share information about your children by providing copies of notices from school, information about upcoming events, and accomplishments of the children. This includes information about extracurricular activities and sports.
- ☞ Purchase a fax machine as well as a photocopier or scanner to make it easier to share information. This may sound like a big purchase, but it's less expensive than a couple of phone calls to your lawyer complaining about communication issues.
- ☞ Make a "parent to parent" folder that can travel back and forth between homes and to and from school. Keep adult issues and concerns in sealed envelopes.
- ☞ If face-to-face or telephone conversations between parents is especially problematic, try e-mail, letters, or a family website or blog.
- ☞ Always act businesslike in communicating with the other parent. Remember, you are in the business of parenting! If you wouldn't speak that way to a business associate, then don't speak that way to the other parent. It is a simple fact of life that we all occasionally have to deal with people we don't especially care for or respect. Deal with it.

- Never send a letter or an e-mail that you wrote while you were angry.
- When communicating by letter or in any writing, don't resort to inflammatory remarks or "fighting words." Do several draft letters and proofread the final one, again.
- Acknowledge the other parent's good deeds or acts of kindness, no matter how small. By "rewarding" good behavior, you are likely to see more of it.
- Set up certain times to talk; in other words, make phone appointments. Try to arrange a time when neither parent will be distracted or interrupted and make sure that the children are not within earshot.
- Resolve one issue at a time and then end the conversation. Do not move beyond the issue at hand because sooner or later an issue will come up that will end in an argument or an unproductive manner. It is best to hang up on a good note after resolving an issue. Adhering to this practice builds positive momentum for future talks and resolution of issues.
- Calling while in the car or on a cell phone can have certain benefits. If things are getting heated or you become too nervous or uncomfortable, you can always say, "I am sorry, you're breaking up. I'll call you later" or try "Can you hear me now?" This is an easy out if you need to regroup or if you are losing momentum in the conversation.
- Keep an organized log or binder of all communication between parents for future reference, if needed.
- Avoid hot topics and sarcasm (yeah, right).
- Have an agenda and stick to it. Stay focused on what you want to accomplish or discuss.
- Try tape recording your end of the conversation and listen to it later to see how you could have been a more effective listener or communicator. The purpose here is to listen to *your-*

self; you don't even need to record your ex's end of the conversation.

Communication Don'ts

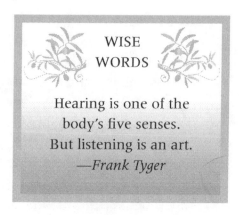

WISE WORDS

Hearing is one of the body's five senses. But listening is an art.
—*Frank Tyger*

- ➣ Don't provide opportunities for disagreement; if the time, place, or manner is not appropriate, exercise your right to remain silent.
- ➣ Don't always have the last word.
- ➣ Don't place emphasis on the other parent.
- ➣ Don't engage in general conversation, other than superficial pleasantries, such as hello and good-bye.
- ➣ Don't resort to name calling, insults, dirty looks, or inappropriate gestures. (Here's a tip: the reverse middle finger extension should be avoided when non-verbal communication is utilized.)

From occasional blaming and bad-mouthing to full-fledged brainwashing, there is a whole continuum of inappropriate behavior that parents often play out at the expense of their children's mental well-being. If you are behaving in such a fashion, STOP! If you're on the receiving end, I encourage you to read *Divorce Poison* by Dr. Richard A. Warshack, author of *The Custody Revolution*. After reading *Divorce Poison* you will be able to distinguish different types of criticism, ranging from occasional mild bad-mouthing to severe and systematic brainwashing. You will know how and why parents manipulate their children. You will learn how to detect subtle psychological maneuvers and various guises. Most importantly, you will discover powerful strategies to preserve or rebuild loving relationships with your children.

Remember, every time you refer to your ex-spouse in a negative way it just keeps the anger alive. So, just say no! Don't do it. Learn to deal with your ex and move on emotionally. Life is short and a happy childhood is a terrible thing to miss. If you stay angry, you will miss it.

Empower Yourself

You may have seen language in court orders that seems ridiculous. Provisions that tell parents to "be nice" should really not be necessary. However, from time to time they do serve as useful reminders. (For more "nice-nice" language to be used in parenting agreements and court orders see appendix A.) Here's one good example of such language that highlights a worthy goal:

> Above all, we want our children to know that, regardless of the decisions made, they are not to be misinterpreted or in any way diminish the love that we have for them. With this in mind, we agree that neither parent shall do anything, nor permit anyone else to do anything, that may estrange our children from the other parent, or injure the opinion or bond as to both, mother and father.

Communication is hard enough to master in a loving and committed relationship. In the context of separation and divorce, it becomes a matter of your willingness to change for the sake of your children. If you really desire to empower yourself by understanding the dynamics of communicating with a difficult co-parent and mastering communication techniques that work for most parents in conflict, you should attend mediation training or co-parenting classes. You can consult your city or county court clerk's office for information on family law or co-parenting seminars or workshops. Be willing to learn from others who have been through it or who have counseled others through these difficult times.

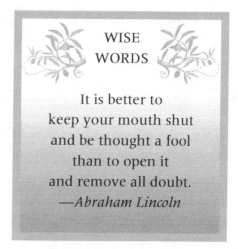

WISE WORDS

It is better to keep your mouth shut and be thought a fool than to open it and remove all doubt.
—*Abraham Lincoln*

Steven R. Covey, in his best-selling book *The Seven Habits of Highly Effective People*, writes that if he had to choose the single most important thing he's learned in the field of interpersonal relations, it would be this: "Seek first to understand, then to be understood."

12

Telephone Contact with the Children

The inability to have meaningful telephone contact with their children can be a significant source of frustration and stress for separated and divorced parents. In fact, trouble with telephone contact occurs surprisingly often. Some of the common complaints sound like this:

- No one returns my calls.
- The other parent hovers over our child during telephone conversations with me.
- They have caller ID and the children are not allowed to pick up the phone if they see my number.
- When I am able to get through, I am told that they are "busy" or they will have to call me back, and they never do.
- I leave messages for my child but she tells me that they are never given to her.

- ☞ My child is very quiet and "non-conversational" when her dad is in the room.
- ☞ My children and I have no privacy during phone calls.
- ☞ The court order says that I am supposed to have reasonable, liberal, and regular phone contact, and I am not getting it.
- ☞ When I call to speak to my children, my ex always gets on the line and starts an argument.
- ☞ I feel like I have to go through gatekeepers just to be able to speak to my children.
- ☞ I should be allowed to talk to my children at least once a day.
- ☞ I can always hear my ex in the background, bad-mouthing me and interrupting my phone call.
- ☞ My ex is doing this just to annoy me.

When Ralph and Stacey separated, their three sons were ages five, nine, and eleven. These angry parents engaged in approximately four years of knock-down, drag-out, ugly custody and visitation litigation. The issue of telephone contact between Ralph and his children created many serious problems that continued to keep the flames ignited between Ralph and Stacey.

From Ralph's perspective, there was no reason why he should not be "allowed" to speak to his children every day at least once. Furthermore, he deemed the breakup of the marriage to be all Stacey's fault and his hostility toward her was present in each and every communication that the two of them had since the separation. Stacey was clearly blocking phone contact between Ralph and his children, but Ralph did nothing to help the situation. He would call repeatedly and leave messages over and over again. Each time he would become more and more frustrated, upset, and aggressive.

Each house was equipped with caller ID and great efforts were made by Ralph to call from different numbers or to block his number from caller ID detection. Those efforts were largely unsuccessful and simply continued to frustrate Ralph, which in turn fanned the flames and kept the lines of dysfunctional communication ablaze. Ralph, like many parents in similar situations, failed to realize that children generally have little to say about their

TRUCE

Truce is better
than friction.

daily activities, feelings, and future plans *in person*, much less over the telephone. When there are parental complications thrown into the mix, children tend to withdraw simply to avoid the awkwardness of it all. Do you blame them?

Whenever Stacey picked up the phone, Ralph would cuss her out and otherwise belittle and ridicule her. She, in turn, would hang up on him and refuse to take any further calls from him. On the rare occasion that he would get through to speak to one of the boys, he would invariably ask them to either put their mother on the phone or relay messages to their mother and in each and every case, nothing productive ever followed.

It's easy to see that the phone contact between the father and his boys was strained at best — in part, because when Ralph would speak to the children he would badger them about the fact that he left so many messages. Furthermore, he would remind them that their mother would not let them speak to him. This took away from the limited time they had together and it kept the children squarely in the middle of parental squabbling.

In many cases, the real issue is not about one's inability to speak with the children or the loss to the children of such brief telephone conversations, but something much more complex. This *something* must be put into proper perspective in order to avoid a constant and nagging reminder of the unnecessary parental conflict that can linger on and adversely affect each parent's relationship with their children.

In attempting to deal with these types of issues, it is helpful to ask a key question of yourself before choosing what course of action to take: Is the issue really about the benefit of telephone contact or is it a test of wills between me and my ex?

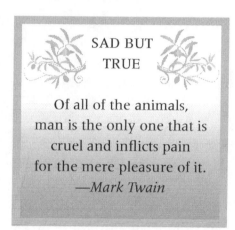

SAD BUT TRUE

Of all of the animals, man is the only one that is cruel and inflicts pain for the mere pleasure of it.
—*Mark Twain*

This is a key question, and it can be asked of any dispute. When you find yourself continually fighting about the same thing, ask yourself whether you're really fighting for the benefit of the children or whether you're trying to exercise power or control over the other parent.

Here are a few key reminders and suggestions.

- ☞ Generally speaking, children do not have a lot to say when they are on the telephone with adults no matter where they live or who they are with.
- ☞ When you do speak to your children by phone, keep the conversation short and sweet.
- ☞ Do not ask your child to relay any message to the other parent. If you are intending to speak to the other parent, you should not do so in the same telephone conversation. Make a separate telephone call or appointment to discuss parental issues when the children are not within earshot.
- ☞ Do not put the responsibility on the children to call you. Period. Let them be children.
- ☞ In some cases it may be appropriate to purchase a cell phone for your children. There are special phones that allow only

for pre-programmed in-coming and outgoing phone calls, which the parents can set. Perhaps a separate house line would be a worthwhile option to consider.

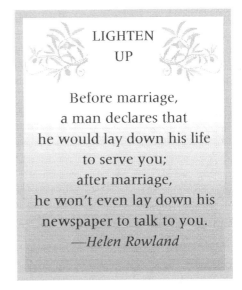

LIGHTEN UP

Before marriage,
a man declares that
he would lay down his life
to serve you;
after marriage,
he won't even lay down his
newspaper to talk to you.
—*Helen Rowland*

- Explore other means of communication, such as e-mail, text messaging, video cam, and so forth. Family blogs or websites may also help promote parent-child communication and interaction.

- *Do not do unto the other parent as that parent does to you.* By this benevolent ideal, I mean that even if your efforts are intentionally frustrated by the other parent when you try to speak to your children by telephone, do not respond in kind.

- When your children are with you, you should arrange for them to call the other parent at reasonable intervals. Be considerate; leave the room and give them privacy. And, do not inquire about their conversation. Teach your children that you are not attempting to frustrate communication with their other parent and that you will not interrogate them on such matters.

If your telephone efforts are being thwarted, you need to let it go, or at least put it into perspective and realize that the children will be okay if they do not hear from you for a few days and vice versa. Telephone contact issues are generally blown out of proportion. There are plenty of ways to let children know that they are always in your thoughts and that you care about them. Furthermore, when you do next see your children, remember that it's a real "downer" for them if you grill them about the lack of telephone contact.

The best way to combat telephone communication issues is for *both parents* to recognize that telephone contact is generally a good thing if it is conducted in a proper fashion. Both parents should do everything that they can to encourage meaningful and productive telephone contact. However, the nature and duration of telephone contact should be kept simple. A quick or passing phone call to say "hello," "I love you," or "I'll look forward to seeing you soon" are really all that is needed to remind the children that they are thought of with love and affection when they are not physically with you.

JUST A TIP

If you and your ex need to have a phone conversation, the best way to control what your child hears or does not hear is to set a time to speak to the other parent when the child is with you. That way, you can direct when and where the conversation takes place. You can also be assured that your child is not within earshot of the conversation.

Focus on how you will spend your time with your children. Each and every time that you are with your children you should embrace those moments as wonderful opportunities to share and experience unconditional love and recognize it as a gift from God. Do not waste those precious moments on squabbling over unreturned telephone calls and things that really do not matter.

The suggestions for telephone contact, like many of the suggestions and techniques in this book, have a common theme when it comes to changing or modifying parental behavior — a bit of the "monkey see, monkey do" approach. Of course, you could also call it the Golden Rule. Even in the most contentious and difficult cases, it makes a difference if one parent chooses to lead or teach *by example*, despite the temptation to fight fire with fire. Once you set a pattern of conduct and stick to it, the other parent's counterproductive efforts will eventually tire, especially when you send the message that they are no longer getting to you.

The Peanut Gallery

Separation and divorce are by no means simply private matters. It is more than likely that somebody you know has reportedly been screwed by a former spouse, a biased judge, an incompetent lawyer, or any combination thereof. The stories about who said what, who did what, and who got what are as similar and as unique as the people who listen to them. Surely you know someone who has been through an ugly divorce.

When parties separate, everyone seems to have an opinion. Gossip and rumors will run rampant upon the separation of even the most likely of couples to part company. When the otherwise "perfect couple" forgets "until death do us part," loyalty conflicts may be even more likely to arise among family and friends. Worse yet, everyone will share their opinions and advice whether requested or not.

Wanna-be lawyers and even many licensed attorneys are quick to "advise" potential litigants how to jockey for position, whether by hiding money and assets, dictating the type and frequency of child visitation "to allow," or in taking one to the proverbial cleaners. Who should you listen to? Will what worked for this one or that one work for you? How can you prove your case?

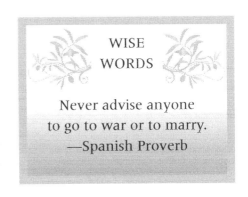

WISE WORDS

Never advise anyone to go to war or to marry.
—Spanish Proverb

Who will testify on your behalf? Will you have to go to court? For what? When? How? Why?

Everyone who has ever come into contact with either of the estranged parties is a potential witness. Some will promise to gladly testify about first-hand observations of the couple when they were "together." The desire to produce adverse testimony will likely include "reluctant witnesses" too. Those who say that they do not want to get involved may be served a subpoena to come to court to testify about the behavior, activities, or some dastardly allegations of at least one of the parties.

The attacks are usually well plotted and planned. However, even those who want to come to your aid will likely not say what you think they will say when they are in the hot seat. The witness chair is an intimidating place to be. More often than not, even the most favorably biased witnesses will overcompensate by trying to appear fair and impartial. The witnesses that go out of their way to "bury" the other side are usually just discounted as being too aligned with one of the parties. In general, your witnesses are expected to praise you and to trash the other party, either directly or indirectly. This is no secret, and trust me — the judges have figured this out too! So trust me on this too: it is far better to accentuate your positive parenting than to constantly attack and demean the other side.

Separation and divorce undoubtedly redefine the nature of one's associations, not only with his or her former spouse and children, but often with other family members, friends, associates, acquaintances, and with people in general. When people are in the midst of moderate to high levels of separation anxiety and stress is

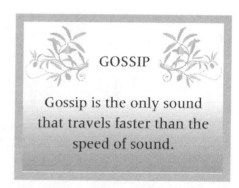

GOSSIP

Gossip is the only sound that travels faster than the speed of sound.

high, everyone who interacts with them can feel the tension. If you know anyone currently in the midst of an ugly divorce, you may have already come to realize that those issues are all that this person can talk about. It is consuming.

Sure, at times everyone needs someone to talk to and confide in. And, everyone needs to seek advice from time to time. However, when it comes to separation and divorce (especially with acrimonious child custody and access disputes), many people will get caught up in the "three-foot principle." What is that you ask? Basically, anyone that comes within three feet of them will not be able to escape without listening to the whole saga, again and again. The separation issues of the "three footer" somehow always become the only topics of any conversation — no matter the time, place, or setting. Soon this otherwise sociable and likable person will be avoided by family and friends for fear of being "trapped." It is kind of like the person who gets involved in a network marketing business opportunity — one that recruits other sales associates with the hope of making a percentage off of them and their future "would-be" sales force. Did someone say MLM (multi-level marketing)? Just like those people who use every conversation as an introduction to their sales pitch, parents in the midst of custody chaos are also known for getting on the nerves of others.

Whether you are this "possessed" person stuck in the throes of divorce, or you know someone who currently fits the mold, it is good to recognize that a certain amount of self-absorbing, all-consuming focus on one's transitional situation is quite natural. It is a necessary stage to pass along the path of separation and divorce. It is a place on the way to acceptance and recovery. However, it needs to

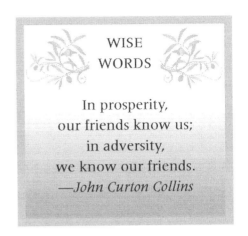

WISE
WORDS

In prosperity,
our friends know us;
in adversity,
we know our friends.
—*John Curton Collins*

pass as quickly as it can. If you do not regroup quickly, you will, beyond any reasonable doubt, be guilty of negatively impacting many of your most important interpersonal relationships.

I could share many incidents of my own personal, family, social, and business encounters where I was less than pleasant to those around me when I felt that they did not understand what I was going through or when I was offered "advice" that I felt was contrary to my beliefs, values, and overall objectives. If that's you, eventually those with whom you share close, friendly, and loving relationships may not want to be around you. The actions, reactions, words, and body language of others may be a sign that they have heard enough about your situation. You need to be aware of this.

It is no great revelation that there is much negativity associated with people going through adult separation anxiety. Harness that negative drive and focus it on proactive and productive endeavors. If you won't do it for yourself, you need to do it for your children. They are like sponges. They absorb our outward expressions whether we recognize it or not. Parents surrounded by negativity are not nearly as effective at parenting as their children require and deserve.

14

Maintaining a Positive Mental Attitude

Maintaining a positive mental attitude, or PMA, is such an important and often overlooked component of child custody litigation that I feel compelled to give you a few resources that can at least introduce you to things that are available. These resources can give you the boost that you will need from time to time. Whether in the form of books, tapes, CDs, websites, or whatever, find some sources of inspiration and motivation. Put the headphones on, pop in a tape or CD, and take a walk. While sitting in traffic, learn. If you can't sleep, read. Fill the self-talk that goes on in your head with useful information. Bitching and moaning gets old and it wears you out. You need to regroup. The time is now.

Here are some of my favorite motivational personalities:

- Earl Nightingale
- Tony Robbins
- Brian Tracy
- Les Brown
- Stephen Covey
- Zig Zigler

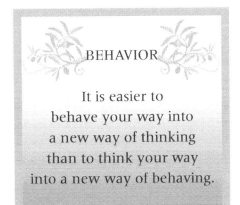

BEHAVIOR

It is easier to behave your way into a new way of thinking than to think your way into a new way of behaving.

Yet even more than these personalities, I truly admire Oprah Winfrey. It seems to me that while Oprah's overall objective is indeed to empower people, she strives to help people see themselves differently, look at who they really are, and learn from others who have done well and accomplished their dreams. As one of the most influential women in the world, Oprah continues to use her talk show for issues that are important to her. If calming child custody chaos was an Oprah topic, there might be some needed change at an accelerated pace. That would be a good thing. I would really like to meet Oprah one day. If you know anyone who could help arrange that, please let me know!

Use the Resources That Work for You

There are countless resources along the path to self-improvement. A quick trip to the local Barnes and Noble self-improvement section may hold the key to your life-changing opportunity. One way to look at the challenges that lie ahead is to welcome them as growth opportunities. You are probably thinking, "Yeah right," but in a few years when much of the adjustment is behind you, I hope you will agree.

Going to seminars can be very therapeutic. It gives you a chance to focus for a few hours, to be entertained to some degree, and to meet new people. Sometimes it helps just to keep an open mind and to fill it with new perspectives. The mere act of learning something new is a great distraction from wallowing in the same old divorce and custody conflict. For a variety of useful self-improvement resources, see appendix F as well as my blog, www.DivorceWithoutDishonor.com.

Whether you asked for it or not, your life is changing in significant ways. In the end, you can and will be a better person. You will build character and hopefully be an inspiration to your children. Being a positive living example is a major part of parenting and it should be a constant goal, no matter how much things change. The example you set and the paths you take are all up to you.

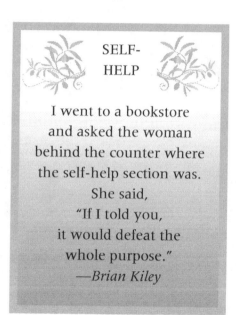

SELF-HELP

I went to a bookstore and asked the woman behind the counter where the self-help section was. She said, "If I told you, it would defeat the whole purpose."
—*Brian Kiley*

15 Support Groups

Single parenting can be a lonely and difficult road, but it doesn't have to be. Community is essential. It can help carry you to the high road when you're feeling worn out and overwhelmed. Support groups for single parents often provide just the help that's needed. One great resource in the form of a nationally recognized support group is Divorce Care. About eighteen months after my separation, I received a letter at my law office introducing a new resource in our community — an upcoming Divorce Care seminar/support group, which was being held at a local church. It was not an invitation to join the church, contribute money, or buy anything.

The letter had obviously been sent to attorneys in the area to introduce a potential resource for their clients. Along with the letter were brochures introducing the upcoming divorce recovery seminars. The program was described as a new video series featuring some of the nation's foremost experts on divorce and recovery topics. The video seminars were promoted in conjunction with support group discussions of the materials presented during the videos. They even offered to provide childcare for children up to the fifth grade. It was a

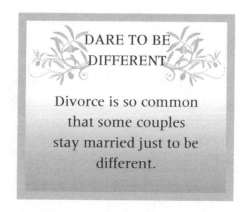

DARE TO BE DIFFERENT

Divorce is so common that some couples stay married just to be different.

great program and it has grown a lot since I went through my trying times.

Divorce Care seminars and support groups are led by people who understand what you are going through and want to help. You'll gain access to valuable Divorce Care resources to help you deal with the pain of the past and rebuild your life with an eye toward a brighter future.

Some of the topics covered in Divorce Care include:

- Why divorce hurts so much; how to stabilize your life
- The road to healing/finding help — understanding your losses and steps to healing
- Facing your anger — identifying the causes of your anger and reducing your anger
- Facing your depression — understanding your depression and how it can help you heal
- Facing your loneliness — effective ways to deal with your loneliness and mistakes to avoid when feeling lonely
- What does the owner's manual say?
- Why the Bible is important; finding God's help and guidance
- New relationships — when are you ready for a new relationship? Keys to successful relationships

- Financial survival — how to stabilize financially and develop a survival plan
- Kidcare — understanding the effects of divorce on children; tips on being an effective single parent
- Single sexuality — understanding sexuality from God's perspective; being single and satisfied
- Forgiveness — the danger of not forgiving; how to know if you have forgiven
- Reconciliation — understanding what reconciliation is and is not; how it happens
- Moving on, growing closer to God — understanding the good that can come from your divorce; defining what is at the center of your life

CHILD PSYCHOLOGY

Child psychologists have discovered many excellent rules for bringing up other people's children.

My Divorce Care experience was invaluable. More than a decade has passed since I used their resources, but Divorce Care is still there and it has grown significantly. The Divorce Care facilitators understand just how deeply individuals and families are hurt by divorce. There are thousands of Divorce Care divorce recovery support groups meeting throughout the United States, Canada, and nearly twenty other countries and territories. There's one near you! If you can't find a Divorce Care group near you or it's not the right fit for some reason, keep looking. So many resources are available.

When I attended the program, my main man was just three years old. I went every week, religiously. On a few occasions I took Nicholas with me along with his sack of toys, games, and snacks.

Even though he wanted me to stay in the playroom with him, he had fun with the other children while I went to the program and I was glad he was close by. There is something about looking at your child and knowing that to him, you are everything, that makes all the effort worthwhile. During those times, the inspiration to care for him carried me to a better place.

LIGHTEN
UP

An old man
went to a wizard
to ask him if he could
remove a curse that
he been living with for
the last forty years.
The wizard said,
"Maybe, but you will have to
tell me the exact words
that were used to put the
curse on you."
The old man said
without hesitation,
"I now pronounce you man
and wife."

16 Relocation Issues

As if it isn't hard enough for children to lose the stability of having both parents living under the same roof, it is really traumatic when one parent moves far away from the other. Often, such a plan is kept secret until such time as a move is basically not preventable by the adversely affected parent. It's one thing when the non-custodial parent makes the choice to move further away from their children. It's quite another set of circumstances when the parent with whom the children primarily reside unilaterally decides to move across the country with the children. These types of cases are difficult for everyone.

I can think of only a few good reasons to move far away from the children's familiar surroundings: a once-in-a-lifetime job opportunity that can significantly improve the likelihood of success for the children, to be close to an elderly or ill parent or family member, or to live in a witness protection program during a mob trial. Those reasons aside, there are usually many more compelling reasons *not* to move far away from your children's other parent. Generally speaking, if a parent has sole legal custody of their minor children, the children will usually live with that parent for the majority of time.

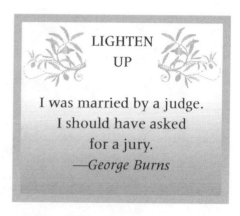

LIGHTEN
UP

I was married by a judge.
I should have asked
for a jury.
—*George Burns*

Occasionally, you may see a 50-50 time-sharing arrangement, with one parent having final decision-making authority. In either situation, the laws of most states do not afford the non-custodial parent with much ability to prevent an out-of-state move.

Many states have laws on the books that require a custodial parent to give written notice of one's intent to relocate a child out of state when there is a current court order in place regarding child custody and visitation. Whether it is sixty days or six months, there is generally nothing under the law that prohibits a parent from moving out of state — other than the terms of a governing court order that specifically addresses the situation. While one can be found in contempt of court for disobeying the terms of a court-ordered schedule, this will be of little consolation after the relocation has taken place. Let's look at a few scenarios.

Let's assume that there is a legitimate reason for the mother to strongly consider a move. Perhaps her employer is opening a new branch office and she is the best-qualified candidate. Maybe she is also fortunate enough to obtain a huge salary increase and move to an area that affords her child all kinds of financial, educational, and social opportunities. Assume further that she has remarried and her child and his step-dad, a house husband, also share a wonderful relationship. In fact, let's throw in a new baby brother for the youngster that he also adores.

Suppose that since the divorce this mother has not done anything to alienate the child from the father. She cooperates in following the letter and spirit of the court order and she keeps her exhusband fully informed of all

CHANGE

When you want to change the circumstances, you must first change your thinking.

child-related matters. Once she fully considers the opportunity to move, she provides her ex-husband with written notice in accordance with the law and explains all of her reasons for wanting to move. Suppose too, that she has voluntarily agreed to provide the father with additional time in the summer, more of the holidays, and to pay for airfare and transportation costs for their son to continue to enjoy a meaningful relationship with his dad.

In such a case, if the child's father does not agree to the proposal, there is little that he can do to prevent the move from happening. If he files for an emergency hearing with the court, it may be denied. In the eyes of the courts, an emergency usually must mean some immediate irreparable harm is about to be done to the child or something is about to occur, which is patently contrary to the child's best interests. A petition to modify custody and visitation could be filed based on the "change of circumstances" that will now be occurring. However, in many jurisdictions, due to the backlog of cases, by the time such a case comes up for trial, the move will have long taken place. The standard of review will be whether there have been material changes in circumstances that affect the minor child. In an out-of-state move, that is a relatively easy threshold. However, once a material change of circumstances is demonstrated, the court will essentially weigh all of the factors that it normally considers when making a custody determination. In this scenario, the child will end up residing with his mother in their new home state.

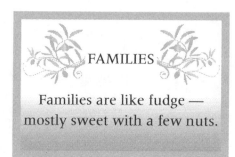

FAMILIES

Families are like fudge — mostly sweet with a few nuts.

Now let's consider scenario number two. In Donna's case, she thought that she had it in the bag when she chose to move from Maryland to Texas. From her "perspective" she would be well within her authority of temporary custody if she moved herself and her child to Texas *before* the final divorce and custody trial date. She and her husband went through an ugly separation and ever since her husband moved out, Donna jerked him around repeatedly about seeing their six-year-old son, Tyler. Donna's husband, Jake, made matters harder for himself by threatening her, calling her names, and leaving nasty messages on Donna's answering machine.

Jake was furious; he thought that he had lost for sure. This dad knew that if he got jerked around when he and his ex lived twenty minutes apart, he would essentially be cut out of Tyler's life once his son moved to Texas. Truth be told, that was what Donna wanted. Donna was pretty smart and quite manipulative, and she played Jake like a drum. Donna waited until the summer to move, and with the temporary court order she had authority to enroll Tyler in the Texas school system. She knew that the court case wasn't scheduled until late November and by then Tyler would already be settled and presumably doing well. She would be extra accommodating and tell Jake that he could come whenever he wanted and that she would even split airfare and hotel accommodations. She promised to be fair in working out all the holidays and allow Jake to spend a week or two in the summer with their son.

Unfortunately for her, the trial judge had seen her type many times before. The reasons that she gave for relocating were that her fiancé had a wonderful job offer with the Exxon Oil Company, her sister lived there and could help with child care while Donna looked for a new job and a

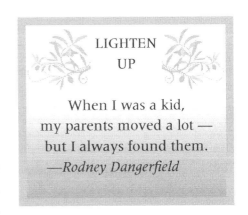

LIGHTEN UP

When I was a kid, my parents moved a lot — but I always found them.
—*Rodney Dangerfield*

fresh start, there were many young children in the community, and the school she had chosen for Tyler was right down the street from her new house. The yard was big and there were plenty of activities for children available in her new community. In addition, she stated that all of the turmoil between her and her husband was not good for Tyler and if she and Jake did not have to deal with each other as often, Tyler would be better off. Lastly, Tyler just adored Billy Bob, her fiancé whom she met six months ago. The fact that she made this move before trial and against Jake's wishes did not sit well with the judge.

Three years later, Tyler is doing great. He has many friends and is doing well in school. He is active in sports and he and his dad have a wonderful relationship. Every other Thanksgiving weekend, winter break, spring break, and for two whole weeks in the summer, Tyler gets to travel to Texas to spend time with his mother and Billy Bob!

There are many possible fact patterns and hypothetical situations that fall between the two extremes illustrated here and many possible outcomes. However, none of them are ever easy to litigate, decide, or live through. In all relocation cases there is a cost-benefit analysis that is undertaken by the parties, their attorneys, and the court. In its most fundamental terms, the basis for the decision is simply whether the move is more important and beneficial to the child than the current relationship the child has with the non-moving party. Sadly, the people most affected generally have the least input into the equation.

Of course, I have a strong opinion on this issue. I do not think that the path to Big Rock can lead too far from a child's home. Having seen the effect on parents and children alike, I can only imagine the pain that any loving and involved parent would feel if their children were essentially pulled away from them by the other parent's choice to move. Forget what the law says and allows for a moment. Don't we as parents have a moral obligation to do all that we can so that our children have the opportunity and benefit of as much of each parent's time, attention, and love as can be practically accomplished? I think we do.

Quite frankly, an unnecessary move (or one designed to frustrate the other parent's relationship with their children) is not just unfair to the other parent, it is downright dirty. It is almost like thievery and not far down the continuum from child abduction. No decent parent should plan on moving far away from the children's other parent, outside of extraordinary circumstances. Even then, great safeguards should be implemented to counterbalance the inherent loss and unfairness to the child. There are some personal sacrifices that simply have to be made when you are a separated or divorced parent. Staying close by is generally one of them. There are exceptions to this ideal, but not many.

The decision to relocate a substantial distance from your children's other parent should not be taken lightly. Even after separation and divorce, many decisions that you make about your life will substantially impact your child's relationship with the other parent.

17

Money, Money, Money
Child Support Issues

C hild support should not be measured in dollars alone. Child support, in its truest sense, encompasses not only monetary support but the right and obligation of a parent to support their child morally, physically, emotionally, and spiritually. Under "the law," child support and visitation are separate issues, but in practice they are often intertwined. If a non-custodial parent, usually the dad, is not being permitted to see his children, he is far less likely to fulfill his monetary child support obligations. When moms are not getting the financial support that they are entitled to under the law, there is often a temptation to withhold visitation or otherwise use the children to punish the non-compliant obligor.

It is no secret that child support is predominately based on the income of both parents. But there are other factors considered in the calculation of child support: the residential schedule of the children, health insurance payments, before- or after-school care, daycare, private schooling, extraordinary medical expenses, and even transportation costs for visitation in some cases. Over my many years of interacting with men who feel that their child support obligations are unfair, oppressive, or unwarranted, I have become convinced that those parents who constantly scheme, plot,

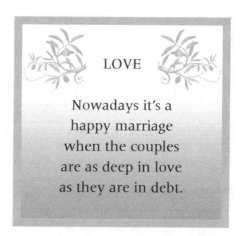

LOVE

Nowadays it's a happy marriage when the couples are as deep in love as they are in debt.

and plan on how they will hide their true income not only cheat their children but they also do themselves a great disservice.

When parents go out of their way to impoverish themselves, if not in fact, then at least on paper, for purposes of minimizing child support payments, they often fail to realize or care how much it costs to raise a child. Their children may be deprived of many material things and, unfortunately, that often does not seem to matter. Similarly, opportunities for their children to participate in some activities or events are also compromised when parents do not pay what they should in monetary support. This particular segment of disgruntled parents views child support as an undeserved windfall to their ex and nothing else.

The effort and energy that some people spend attempting to avoid or lessen their child support responsibilities is astonishing. Those who are really serious about not contributing to the custodial parent's financial resources often choose to live in their parents' basement, shack up with roommates, or live in tents before they will pay what they are supposed to pay in child support. This shirking of parental responsibility is often not out of a lack of love for the children, but it is directly attributable to the hatred or ill will still harbored toward the other parent.

Usually, the money that they supposedly "save" by playing "hide and seek" with their income or earning potential is minimal when compared to the setbacks that they bestow upon themselves. By intentionally showing minimal income, they may limit the opportunity to own a par-

PAY UP

Why is divorce so expensive? Because it's worth it (sometimes).

ticular home, or any home at all. Self-impoverishment negatively affects one's ability to obtain sufficient credit, personal loans, business loans, or other potential means for financial advancement.

It is beyond the scope of this book to get into the facts and figures of child support calculations and the statistical analysis relating to the payment of child support. Suffice it to say that a simple Google search under "child support" will lead you to more than you ever wanted to know on the subject. The Internet provides access to each state's child support guidelines, child support calculators, legal research resources, and resources for laypersons alike. (But you know that, right?)

Regardless of the actual dollar amount mandated by child support "guidelines," there are some basic dos and don'ts that can be helpful in easing the financial tensions that so often spill over into custody and visitation disputes.

Child Support Dos

- Financially support your children.
- Keep financial matters and all other parenting issues as separate as possible.
- Be realistic in your assessment of how much it costs to raise children.

☞ Accept the fact that if you are the one paying child support, the law does not impose any duty upon the recipient to account for the money actually spent directly on the children.

☞ Purchase items for the children (including clothing) for the times that your children are with you. Child support payments are not necessarily intended to cover child-related expenses when the children are with you.

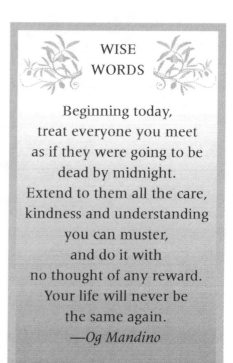

WISE WORDS

Beginning today,
treat everyone you meet
as if they were going to be
dead by midnight.
Extend to them all the care,
kindness and understanding
you can muster,
and do it with
no thought of any reward.
Your life will never be
the same again.
—*Og Mandino*

☞ Spend child support wisely, as it is intended for the use, benefit, and expenses associated with raising children, not as your extra "fun" money.

Child Support Don'ts

☞ Don't make the payment of support, or anything else related to money or property, contingent on child access.

☞ Don't ask for receipts or an accounting of how child support is spent.

☞ Don't discuss child support or adult-to-adult financial matters with your children.

☞ Don't tell your children that they cannot do or have things because the other parent does not pay sufficient support, even if it is true.

⇒ Don't discuss child support or disputed adult financial matters in front of your children.

Count the Cost

Sadly, parents will often spend several months or even years worth of child support money,

LAWYERS

A lawyer is a person who profits by your experience.

which could otherwise be spent directly for the benefit of their children, just fighting over who should have to pay what amount in child support and child-related expenses (reimbursement for medical bills not covered by insurance, school clothes and supplies, and expenses for extracurricular activities for the children). It makes no sense, especially if these types of disputes are handled through lawyers. Regardless of monetary considerations, children need the love, warmth, and positive guidance of both parents, and anything that is said or done to diminish those basic needs is costly — in more than dollars alone. When it comes down to the almighty dollar, whose children would you rather put through college, your own, or your attorney's?

And speaking of college, if you plan on helping your children get there you might want to keep your attorney's fees and litigation expenses to a minimum. Recreational litigation, spending money on lawyers to take unnecessary action just to harass and annoy your former partner, is an expensive proposition. These days parents often feel that sending their children to college is no longer an option they can afford, especially when the high cost of education continues to rise.

When parents separate, plans for the future, and especially your children's future, can require a great deal of extra planning and saving. The financial fallout from divorce has led to a new and growing niche market for financial planners. Financial divorce specialists focus on the financial facts and figures associated with the long-term consequences of financial settlement proposals. One of the many benefits of consulting such professionals is to lessen the time needed to financially "re-group." If you leave financial disputes to be resolved based simply on what you believe is "fair," you may be quite disappointed later on when you crunch the numbers. Remember, numbers don't fib, people do.

18

Transportation Issues

C hances are that since your separation, there have been at least a few arguments about which parent should do the driving (or otherwise arrange transportation) for the children between homes or to and from activities. In fact, if there haven't been any disagreements in this area of parental interaction, you are living the exception.

The basic problem for separated and divorced parents concerning transportation issues often sounds like this: "If you want to see the children, you'll have to pick them up and drop them off, otherwise it isn't happening." Well, I don't know how you react when you're on the receiving end of such directives, but many parents feel a kind of knee-jerk, "kiss my ass" response rise to the surface. Of course, verbalizing such a response doesn't do much for positive parental interaction.

The transportation issues and the messages they send are critical, especially when dealing with children of tender years. In a typical arrangement where dad is picking up the children from mom's residence, there are many problematic scenarios. Let's assume that mom does not welcome dad into the house and is otherwise not thrilled

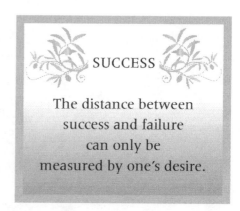

SUCCESS

The distance between success and failure can only be measured by one's desire.

at his presence. He likely waits on the porch. Regardless, he may feel like he gets less respect than a door-to-door salesman.

Since the children are often not ready when dad arrives (whether by chance or by design), it creates tension. Dad may be banging at the door, angry that he has to wait at all. He may be perturbed over the fact that he *had to drive* in the first place. The children may be conveniently smack dab in the middle of video games and aggravated at the "interruption."

Of course, if dad is late, there is a similar but different mounting tension inside the house. And, if dad shows up early, there are still issues. Mom may outwardly and openly, or even unwittingly, show her agitation. Regardless of exactly what sparks it, there is ample opportunity for unnecessary dialogue to take place in front of the children. You may think that children don't pay attention to what's going on, but you know you're fooling yourself, right?

Another uncomfortable situation for the children is the "hello and good-bye" part of the front porch scenario. When the children know that mom and dad do not like each other, they are in a lose-lose situation. At this inopportune time parents may try to capture the attention of the children or otherwise jockey for affection. These face-to-face transition times are a perfect opportunity to "show off," and the parent with "home court advantage" will likely "win." Everyone else, including the departing children, will lose.

This loyalty turmoil is a disaster for the children. When parents deliberately try to use the affections of their children in front of the other parent, whether to feel important or special in their own right, or to make that point to the parent on the porch, it is cruel and not truly affectionate at all. Children see right through it, even the very young.

If the face-to-face front porch pick-up went badly, it is usually followed by an unpleasant and uncomfortable car ride, especially for the young passengers. It does not have to be that way. A simple solution like sharing transportation in a certain manner can prevent most of the problems and transform the transition into a healthy experience for the children.

To not share the transportation that enables your children to spend time with both parents is actually unfair. While it is not often thought about, transportation at transition times sends messages that affect the way children view each parent. So let's look at a few transportation dos and don'ts.

Transportation Dos

☞ The parent who is currently spending time with the children is responsible for transporting them to the other parent. In doing so, the driving parent has the ability to arrive in a timely fashion and say his or her good-byes in the car. Unless the child is of very tender years, the parent doing the driving can simply remain in the car. The other parent can wait at his or her front door. The children can have their private and meaningful good-byes in the car and likewise they can be emotionally free upon entering their other home. There is very little opportunity for unpleasant conversation, remarks, or dirty looks. No one is caught in the middle of anything. Even a door slam has little meaning or effect and is, therefore, unlikely to occur.

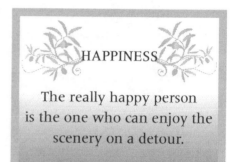

HAPPINESS

The really happy person is the one who can enjoy the scenery on a detour.

Another major benefit to this method is the wonderful subliminal message that comes with it. By taking your children to be with their other parent, to a certain extent you are expressing approval of that relationship and taking some responsibility for maintaining it. The driving parent also has the responsibility to make sure that everything that needs to be done prior to departure is completed in a timely fashion. Remember, when you are in the driver's seat, you control the process.

Even when you're running late (due to traffic of course!), the parent who is waiting to receive the children is far better off waiting in the comfort of their own home than on your porch feeling belittled — or waiting to be.

☞ Share transportation duties for extracurricular activities in a similar fashion. If there is a game or practice that falls on "your" scheduled time with the children, take them to it. In addition to teaching punctuality, this shows your children that you consider their activities to be important.

☞ Use the time in the car to talk with your children and follow up on any topics or issues you've been discussing at home.

☞ Remind your children they can use the transportation time for reading, homework, or working on a continuing project or hobby.

Consider playing educational audio tapes or CDs; think about learning a foreign language together.

Depending on the traffic and the age of your children, use the time as simple quiet time. Even children sometimes need and welcome some time to just stare out the window and think or to simply "zone out."

JUST
A TIP

Consider playing
educational audiotapes
or CDs in the car;
think about learning a
foreign language together.

Transportation Don'ts

- Don't leave all the driving to one parent.
- Don't object to providing transportation if and when it is for the benefit of your child.
- Don't deny parental access because of transportation disputes.
- Don't intentionally pull up onto the lawn of the other parent and do burnouts.
- Don't drink and drive.

Sharing transportation shows your children that you value their relationship with their other parent. When both parents handle transportation in the same manner, an important sense of consistency is provided. And really, how can anyone realistically argue that equally sharing the transportation for the benefit of one's own children is unfair in any respect?

Stuff

19

Mom bought little Tommy a new Abercrombie and Fitch T-shirt and when he went to "visit" his dad, he was wearing it. When Tommy came back "home," he was wearing an old T-shirt that was too small. Worse yet, that new Abercrombie and Fitch shirt did not make it back. Rest assured that mom will bring it to dad's attention. When she does so, she may even refer to the shirt as "her shirt" since she is the one who paid for it. Dad will be quick to remind her that he pays more child support than he should have to and she should spend more of it on the children rather than on getting her nails done and going out every night. So, from his perspective, he paid for it — so it is *really* his. And, to get one more dig in, he will remind her that when Tommy took his new catcher's mitt to her house, she kept it. It doesn't take much to start a never-ending issue about the children's stuff.

If there are school uniforms and other special clothing that look identical, you may have even resorted to labeling, as many parents do. Little Tommy may even have his white Fruit of the Loom underwear labeled "mom" or "dad" to identify in which home it belongs. Nothing is the child's; everything is mom's or dad's.

CHA-CHING

Remember, talk is cheap... until you hire a lawyer.

Is this happening with your children? One unfortunate result of this kind of thing is that it deprives children of the pride of ownership. Worse yet, it draws them directly into their parents' pettiness. It serves as yet another sad and constant reminder of the dysfunction that surrounds them.

Family law attorneys have to listen to arguments about stuff all the time. When it comes to fighting over children's stuff, one particular father that I represented over a seven- or eight-year period for contempt proceedings, modifications of custody, denial of visitation, protective orders, and the whole gambit of parental disputes, comes to mind. The combatants had each gone through a few attorneys who could not help bring peace to these people. Eventually, mom's lawyer and I began to schedule four-way meetings every so often just to try to resolve something — anything. One particular session was largely about "stuff." In the midst of arguing about who had the blue mittens and who had last year's swimsuits, the other lawyer and I took a break, spoke privately, and developed a plan.

When we reconvened to continue the "list" of mom's purchases and dad's purchases and who had, or allegedly had, the stuff, we just let them argue about it. The dialogue quickly resembled the sound of siblings squabbling. After a lengthy and ugly ruckus about petty "stuff," we told them that they'd collectively just paid close to five hundred dollars in billable hours to have us baby-sit their unproductive discussion. We said that for that kind of money, they could have purchased two or three complete sets of all the "stuff" they were arguing about. At that point they each had that "deer in the headlights" look on their faces. Only after this reality

WISE WORDS

The weak
can never forgive.
Forgiveness is the
attribute of the strong.
—*Indira Gandhi*

check did these parents begin to ease up on the issues related to their children's personal property items.

How can you stop the arguments over your children's personal property? Keeping these three truths in mind should help a bit:

1. Recognize that these items do belong to your children — not to you.
2. Remember that it is not your children's fault that they have to shuffle between parental houses.
3. Help your children to regard both places as "home."

Stuff Dos

☞ If possible, buy at least two of most things to limit the back and forth issues. While the extra expense may seem nonsensical, it is less stressful, more practical, and it can still be much less expensive than fighting over the return of stuff, especially if lawyers are involved.

☞ For common stuff — including basic clothes — try not to worry about what comes back and what doesn't. The clothes are not yours. As long as the children get to wear them, it really won't matter where they are "housed." Really, it won't.

- Try to exchange things in ways that do not regularly involve your children lugging things back and forth.
- Every so often you can arrange pick-up and delivery of large amounts of stuff. Consider occasionally mailing items or using a delivery service; another option is to drop off stuff at the other parent's place of employment or some other agreed upon location, outside of the presence of the children.
- Make exchanges in the parking lot at sports events or other activities. This way things can be transferred from vehicle to vehicle from parent to parent, or by designee, rather than always through the children.
- Designate a special place in each house, such as a box or a basket, to hold things that should go back and forth. This is helpful in limiting the seemingly never-ending search for stuff.
- Recognize that school uniforms, sports uniforms, and special clothing require extra attention and planning. Spares are helpful. Keep an extra uniform in your vehicle for that inevitable special delivery call.
- Avoid having your children lug an overnight bag or other extra stuff to and from school whenever possible. While children of separation and divorce are far more numerous and less stigmatized than in years past, why bring attention to the situation? Students have enough stuff to lug around at school these days. Lugging more stuff simply leaves more opportunity for things to get lost or left behind.
- If you believe a delayed return of a particular item to the other house will be a problem with the other parent, see that it returns in a timely manner. If it's a clothing item, return it laundered.
- For children's birthdays and gift-giving holidays, like Christmas and Hanukkah, communicate directly with each other

about what you're purchasing. Try hard to make some joint gift giving occur.

PARENTS

Children do not cause divorce — parents do.

Stuff Don'ts

- While children need to be taught responsibility for their things, you should not nag your children about where "this" or "that" is located.
- Do not resort to putting labels on clothes and identifying things as "mom's" or "dad's."
- Don't allow your child to feel like a "bag lady" by constantly having to carry around her stuff.
- Don't try to "show up" the other parent by always buying extravagant items or spoiling the children, especially if there is significant economic disparity between parents.
- Don't even think of keeping score of who bought what and what did and did not get "returned" to "your" house or the other house.
- Don't use your children's stuff as your free pass to keep tensions alive with the other parent.
- Do not rely on the other parent to provide you with anything. Prepare for the worst and hope for the best.
- When the children are anywhere within earshot, do not talk about your lack of money or the other parent's spending habits. Children always need stuff. Their shoes wear out and they grow out of clothes and jackets; none of that has anything to do with your separation or divorce.

Realistic Expectations

Most children have a difficult time keeping track of their stuff. Let's face it — many adults do too. In fact, just this morning I couldn't find my car keys. The trouble is that divorce creates a whole new level of problems when it comes to tracking stuff — clothes, toys, games, books, musical instruments, athletic equipment, and everything else your children possess.

JUST A TIP

Designate a special place, such as a box or a basket, to hold things that should go back and forth. This is helpful in limiting the never-ending search for stuff.

One of the best things to do is to remember that your children are *children*. Most children who live in one house can't even successfully keep track of their stuff. "The dog ate my homework" excuse wasn't invented yesterday. Have patience with your children and develop strategies to help them keep track of their stuff and help you keep your frustration level to a minimum.

The "I Gotcha Game"

The ability to leave the concept of unfairness out of parental interaction, for the benefit of your child, is an important milestone along the path to Big Rock. By the time we are old enough to produce children, we should have learned that sometimes life is just not fair. Bad things happen to good people all the time. Some people seem to face much adversity. There are people who deserve better, and there are those who can never seem to have enough good fortune. Sometimes people with little material wealth are rich in spirit, while those who seem to have everything are miserable. It is easy to get hung up on the concept of what is fair and unfair, but this can negatively impact your parenting. Those internal ideals can be a stumbling block when it comes to making child-focused decisions during times of parental turmoil.

One major problem that separated and divorced parents encounter is the difficulty of setting the "unfairness" of the past relationship and the memories of more recent unpleasant interactions with your children's other parent aside when making *current* decisions. I agree. It is difficult. Furthermore, it is much easier to spot "unfairness" when you are the self-proclaimed recipient.

OPINIONS

There are two sides
to every question —
my side and the
wrong side.
—*Oscar Levant*

Often, when one parent believes that the other has recently "screwed" them over on a child-related matter, the old saying of "what goes around comes around" rears its ugly head and turns into the "I Gotcha Game." This "I Gotcha Game" and the whole interrelated "fair and unfair" struggles usually play out when a parent requests anything that has to do with being "permitted" to spend more time with the children. Let's assume that there is a court-ordered schedule in place and that every time you ask the other parent to accommodate the slightest change or deviation, it's refused. It doesn't matter how special the event is or how easy it would be for the other parent to work with you — if he or she wanted to. If, after a while, you routinely feel like you already know the answer before you ask (so that you eventually give up asking), there is the potential to want to retaliate when you get the chance. One day, sooner or later, you will get the opportunity to make a decision to accommodate or frustrate the other parent when he or she needs something from you. This is a classic scenario of using the children as a weapon. Unfortunately, these situations are prevalent, especially in moderate- to high-conflict cases.

It will only take one simple example to illustrate the problems that stem from feelings of being treated unfairly. For instance, let's say you want your children to attend your sister's wedding. It falls on a date that is not your scheduled day with your children. You politely ask the other parent to please accommodate your request; you even offer make-up time or to switch a day.

Here are some typical responses from a parent dwelling on "unfairness":

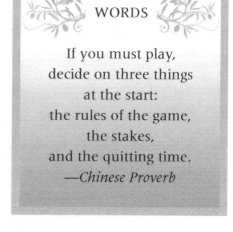

WISE WORDS

*If you must play,
decide on three things
at the start:
the rules of the game,
the stakes,
and the quitting time.*
—*Chinese Proverb*

- ☞ The Nope: *Sorry, it's not your day.*
- ☞ The Stonewall: *I'll have to let you know. I think we have plans that day. (You never get a response, on purpose.)*
- ☞ The Cusser: *F#$! you and your sister.*
- ☞ The Elephant: *Remember when I wanted little Johnny to stay with me an extra day at the beach eight years ago and you said no? Well, I never forget anything, so you know the answer. No.*
- ☞ The Opportunist: *You can, if you agree that I can have an extra week of summer vacation this year and you put it in writing before I give you my answer. Take it or leave it.*

While it's difficult to receive such unfair treatment, the challenge comes when you, the one who is usually shot down, are asked for a similar accommodation. When this opportunity arises, you need to step up to the plate and do the right thing. Don't play the "I Gotcha Game." It is, at times, oh so tempting to just say something like, "Paybacks are a bitch, aren't they?" When you think like that and act accordingly, you are psychologically playing the "I Gotcha Game." You are thinking, "There, I got you, you scumbag. How does it feel?" But this is a game for losers.

It is helpful to ask yourself some child-focused questions when tempted to repay your ex for screwing you over in such situations.

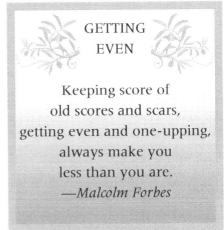

GETTING EVEN

Keeping score of
old scores and scars,
getting even and one-upping,
always make you
less than you are.
—*Malcolm Forbes*

- Should my children be able to do this?
- Will this make me look good or bad in the eyes of a judge?
- Will this make me look good or bad in the eyes of my children?
- If I were asking for this accommodation, what answer would I want to receive?
- What is the big deal if I agree?
- In the scheme of things will it really be of any significance to me later in life?

There are really only two fairness questions that should be considered:

1. Is it fair that your children have to be put in the middle of situations like this?
2. Is it fair (to your children) that you are using them to frustrate their other parent?

When you're tired of the games and it feels like everything is unfair, it might be a good time to consider a Children's Bill of Rights in Divorce, such as this one:

1. The right to be treated as a person and not as a pawn or possession.
2. The right to get emotional support from both parents.
3. The right to spend time with each parent.
4. The right to avoid being caught in the middle.
5. The right to avoid painful games parents play to hurt each other.
6. The right to love each parent without feeling disloyal or guilty.
7. The right to express feelings about the divorce, such as anger, sadness, or fear.
8. The right to remain a child without being asked to take on parental responsibilities.
9. The right to know that they did not cause the divorce.
10. The right to the best financial support that can be provided by both parents.

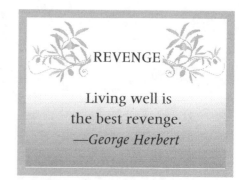

REVENGE

Living well is
the best revenge.
—*George Herbert*

Whether you have been treated badly by your ex or you've been denied time or information or anything else pertaining to your children, don't allow it to be a factor in your decision to accommodate otherwise simple and normal parental requests. The past is past; leave it there. Ask yourself, if we were two *normal* parents, what would we do?

21

Who's Your Daddy

In the summer of 2008 I represented Tom at a settlement conference regarding visitation with his three-year-old son. The other lawyer and I had made great progress that morning. We amicably agreed to expand the father-son parenting schedule, we resolved travel arrangements and transition concerns, and we adjusted the schedule to be more manageable for everyone involved. We even discussed some child support issues without any difficulty. Tom appeared to be unusually jovial that morning. Then, without warning, Tom bellowed, "And I am the only person that will ever be referred to as daddy! Unless you agree to have that put in the court order, there is no deal. I have had it with your shit!"

It went downhill from there, quickly. It appeared that all of our efforts were going to be washed out. Apparently the child's mother had been allowing their son to call the mother's boyfriend "daddy." This was the first time the other attorney or I had heard about it.

As the argument unfolded just outside the judge's chambers, Tom's ex, Donna, retaliated. She criticized Tom for not being around during the first two years of Jack's life. Tom had always contended that Donna did everything to keep him away from Jack; from his perspective, the fact that he had to hire a lawyer and take her to court just to see his son proved that she was a selfish bitch. Tom made his opinions clear. Donna responded in kind, and the expletives flew back and forth for a few moments just before the judge called us in for our settlement conference.

Fortunately, the settlement judge had the appropriate judicial temperament and enough practical experience to resolve the situation. The judge quickly acknowledged Tom's feelings and politely told Donna that he was not there to decide the merits of the allegations but that he agreed with Tom that the child only has one daddy, and that was Tom. He had Donna acknowledge that she would see to it that any confusion that the child had over this issue would be resolved immediately. The judge suggested that perhaps Jack call the boyfriend by his first name or

> ## LIGHTEN UP
>
> A man has six children and is very proud of his achievement. He is so proud of himself that he starts calling his wife "Mother of Six" in spite of her objections. One night, they go to a party. When the man is ready to leave, he shouts at the top of his voice, "Shall we go home, Mother of Six?" His wife, irritated by her husband's lack of discretion. shouts right back, "Any time you're ready, Father of Four!"

Mister Joe or Mr. Smith, or whatever was comfortable, but never, "dad." Tom was beaming as he blurted out, "And I want that spelled out in the court order, Your Honor."

The judge explained why he would *not* allow any such language in a court order. "An order saying that 'Tom is the only person that shall be referred to as daddy' can cause far too many problems," the judge explained. "I am here to help you solve your problems, not give you additional opportunities to find problems." The judge was absolutely correct.

When parents do not get along, you need to limit the things they have opportunities to fight about. A court order containing that sort of language lends itself to future contempt hearings and more "he said-she said" stuff. For example, suppose Tom filed a petition for contempt saying that when he called on the phone to say hello to Jack he heard Donna refer to John, her boyfriend, as Jack's daddy. Tom says that Donna said to Jack, "Say good night to Daddy," while referring to John. Tom is convinced that she did this on purpose just to "set him off." Tom also says he heard John, the boyfriend, laughing in the background. And just that easy, another layer of "he said-she said" is added to the list of problems.

If such nonsense came out in a courtroom, Donna could simply say that she was telling Jack to "say good night to Daddy" in a positive way. That she was referring to Tom, not John, and she was simply encouraging Jack to refer to his father as daddy! As far as John laughing in the background, Donna may respond, "Tom may have heard the television from across the room, but John wasn't even there that night." From Donna's perspective, whether true or not, she may contend that every time she tries to do the right thing, Tom continues to criticize and threaten to take her to court. The bottom line is that no judge wants to hear any of that crap and each party will look equally ridiculous.

In addressing these types of issues, parents should recognize a few truths.

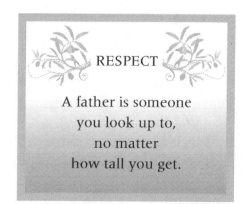

RESPECT

A father is someone
you look up to,
no matter
how tall you get.

- Regardless of what you think of the other parent, your children have only one mom and one dad.
- No one can replace mom or dad.
- For a child to refer to anyone other than his mother or father as "mom" or "dad" is terribly confusing to the child. This includes stepparents too.
- If someone else was being given your special title, you surely wouldn't like it.
- Permitting your children to call your significant other "mom" or "dad" is a sure way to invoke anger and hostility and lessen cooperation. It is also wrong.
- If you are allowing this to happen, you will be looked at with great disfavor by any judge.

By your words and actions you must always convey the message to your children that you recognize that the other parent is equally as special. Your children should naturally feel that way. It is your job (and the other parent's job) to live up to the special title that has been gifted to you.

22
Mother's Day
& Father's Day

Mother's Day and Father's Day is truce time — a free pass. And to get straight to the point, the bottom line is that children belong with their mother on Mother's Day and with their father on Father's Day. Whenever possible it should include an overnight, whether it is Saturday night through Sunday evening or early on Sunday until Monday morning. It needs to happen, period.

Regardless of the case history and no matter how tumultuous the relationship, your children would not even exist without both of you. Parenthood is a gift and at least once a year it does not hurt to demonstrate this fact. When a parent withholds or deliberately interferes with access to the other parent on Mother's Day or Father's Day, it is a sign of real dysfunction. If you are in the middle of custody litigation and the judge learns that you interfered with one of these special days, you will pay the price. On any other day of the year, there can always be "he said-she said" reasons presented about why "visitation" did not occur. However, when it comes to Mother's Day and Father's Day, there is rarely a justifiable excuse in the eyes of the courts.

Last Mother's Day, Mark made a big blunder and the timing could not have been

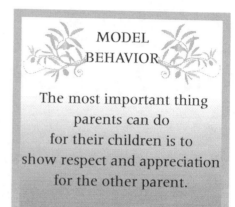

MODEL BEHAVIOR

The most important thing parents can do for their children is to show respect and appreciation for the other parent.

worse — a court date was approaching for the pending modification of custody hearing. Since the divorce, a lot had happened and circumstances had changed. For the past year, the thirteen-year-old boy had lived with dad and the eight-year-old had lived with mom. Brandon, the oldest, refused to live at his mother's house and she had no control over him when he was there. William, however, was a "momma's boy." He loved his mother dearly, and he was comfortable going over his dad's for the weekends. Both boys played baseball and on the night before Mother's Day the boys were both with Mark. Although he said that he intended to take the boys to spend Mother's Day with their mother, it didn't happen.

Brandon had a baseball tournament that Sunday afternoon. Mark assumed that if he took the boys to their mother's house that morning, Donna would either attend and bring the boys, or he would take the boys to the game and they would leave with their mother for the remainder of Mother's Day. As usual, they did not discuss this in advance. The problem was that Donna had no transportation that day and she planned a cookout at her house. She also claimed that she was never told about this game and she rightfully expressed dissatisfaction that there would be a game scheduled on Mother's Day. On Saturday night, when she told Mark that

112

she expected him to drop the boys off to her by 10:00 a.m., he wanted a guarantee that she would take Brandon to his game. He further demanded her assurance that William would go and watch his brother. Donna would not agree. Her punishment? Mother's Day without her children.

> **MOTHERS**
>
> A mother is
> a person who,
> seeing there are only
> four pieces of pie
> for five people,
> promptly announces that
> she never did
> care for pie.

This stunt occurred about two weeks before the court hearing. Donna's lawyer was all over it. It seemed that everything that had happened in the previous year was meaningless; the judge just grilled and blasted Mark about his selfish and childish act. And every time Mark tried to justify it, things just got worse for him. The judge went out of her way to stick it to him and she repeated herself at least five or six times, saying, "There is just no excuse for that!"

None of us should need threatening (and true) stories to remind us that children should be with their mom on Mother's Day and their dad on Father's Day. But when your ex is putting you over the edge and you feel he or she isn't complying with the terms of your agreement, it's easy to lose sight of the obvious. My advice to you is — don't! Don't do things that are likely to make things worse! Or simply: Don't be a jerk!

Mother's Day and Father's Day are opportunities to teach your children to honor their mother and father. It's an idea often forgotten in the aftermath of separation and divorce. If for no other reason, it is important for your children to see that you, too, acknowledge the significance of the other parent in your children's lives. Do everything you can to make the day comfortable for them. Help them prepare to go to their mom or dad's house. Help them choose a gift and give thought to what they appreciate about their other parent.

 JUST A TIP

Help your children pick out a card or small gift for the occasion. You could even help your children with a craft. This will do a lot to ease their confusion and help them feel less torn about these special days.

23 Holidays & Vacations

S cheduling holiday and vacation time with the children can be problematic. Resolving these types of issues can be challenging. Really makes you look forward to them, doesn't it?

The holiday drama that can accompany separation and divorce is illustrated in the little story I will share with you from my experience as a Rainbows facilitator many years ago. Rainbows is a world-recognized and proven program to help children recover after experiencing loss. Rainbows recognizes that a child's grieving process is different from that of an adult's.

I became involved in Rainbows for a few reasons. Yes, I did want to help others and "give back" to the community, but that wasn't my main reason. My worries and concerns were more focused on what life was like, and would be like in the years ahead, for my son. His mother and I continued to battle about virtually everything over which there could be the slightest potential for disagreement. In fact, for us, when it came to vacation planning, we could not even agree how many days there are in a week! (I did suggest that there are seven.)

Rainbows helped me to understand how children perceive loss and how to help them get beyond it with a unique approach of play-based activities. Rainbows teaches how to keep misper-

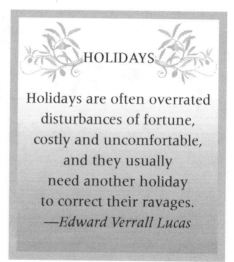

HOLIDAYS

Holidays are often overrated disturbances of fortune, costly and uncomfortable, and they usually need another holiday to correct their ravages.
—*Edward Verrall Lucas*

ceptions and sadness from permanently affecting children. The methods focus on age-appropriate, play-based activities, games, and rituals that have proven to be effective. In addition to benefiting the children it serves, Rainbows parents find comfort and encouragement in trying to help their children during a difficult time in their lives.

I enrolled my son in Rainbows throughout kindergarten and first grade. While he participated in his age-appropriate group, I completed the Rainbows training and volunteered to meet with a group of third graders, mainly to try to understand how all of the parental nonsense looked to them. There were many valuable lessons that those wonderful and surprisingly perceptive children taught me.

One Rainbows memory that still resonates with me to this day illustrates the reality of perception and also the trouble that children of divorce can have during the holidays. At our first meeting after the Christmas holiday, everyone was anxious to tell the group about their Christmas experiences. I will never forget the response that one adorable little girl gave when I asked her what she remembered most about Christmas. She tilted her head and with an innocent smile she said, "It was great all except the part when Mommy wouldn't let Daddy see me and the police had to come over and get me." Before anyone could comment, I suggested that we take a bathroom and water fountain break so that I could dry my eyes in privacy.

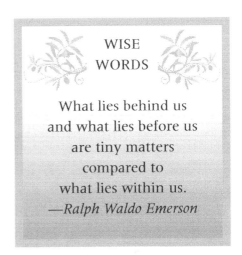

WISE
WORDS

What lies behind us
and what lies before us
are tiny matters
compared to
what lies within us.
—*Ralph Waldo Emerson*

Handling holidays in that fashion is obviously a no-no. There is, however, much you can do to ensure your children's memories of holidays and vacations are good ones. The most basic advice is that when it comes to scheduling holidays and vacations, there needs to be proper planning. As you approach that task, keep in mind that your vacation and holiday time may conflict with the other parent's similar wants and desires. No surprise, right?

Holiday and Vacation Dos

- ➥ Make sure that the holiday and vacation "agreements" are in writing whenever possible.
- ➥ Honor any written or verbal agreements.
- ➥ Give as much notice as possible in requesting a deviation from any prearranged plans.
- ➥ Stay focused on the scheduling issue at hand.
- ➥ Take everyone's work schedules and scheduling restrictions into consideration when trying to draft a holiday or vacation schedule.
- ➥ Make requests, not demands.

- ☞ Say please and thank you.
- ☞ Be flexible if requested to make reasonable accommodations or changes.
- ☞ Be fair.
- ☞ Try to give what you would hope to receive if things were reversed.
- ☞ Provide complete itinerary and contact information to the other parent during any extended stays or out-of-town travel.
- ☞ Make sure that the children call the other parent on holidays when they are with you.
- ☞ Focus your time and energy on how you will spend time with the children when they are with you.
- ☞ Keep a record (for yourself and later on if needed) of all requests that you have made and the results, and all requests the other parent has made and the results.

A Workable Schedule

The objective is to arrive at a written holiday and vacation schedule in an easy-to-follow format so that it can be charted out on your calendar far in advance. Generally, any written agreement or court order should state that the vacation schedule takes precedence over any scheduled holiday as well as the "regular" or primary schedule. Similarly, the holiday schedule overrides the regular schedule.

Make sure that each parent has a complete and full understanding as to what is to take place during any given holiday or vacation period, including beginning and ending times and related transportation issues. Clarify any areas of potential confusion or any possible differing interpretations or understandings as to the dates and times that will deviate from the day-to-day residential schedule.

Perhaps the easiest and fairest way to implement a schedule is an even-odd year approach, with or without a same-day sharing type of schedule. In my experience, parents of younger children usually want to split rather than alternate some holidays.

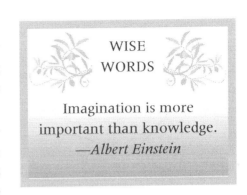

WISE WORDS

Imagination is more important than knowledge.
—*Albert Einstein*

For example, the Thanksgiving holiday always falls on a Thursday and some parents will break up the day so the children can be with mom for part of the day and with dad for part of it too. From the children's perspective, two big meals, maybe two sets of extended families, road travel, and all the hustle and bustle may be less appealing than spending all of Thursday and into Friday with one parent this year and that same designated time frame with the other parent the next year. This is especially advantageous if there is likely to be an argument between the parents as to what time the children should arrive, depart, or return.

For children, Christmas can be even worse when parents break up the day. It is like a rollercoaster with highs and lows coming after the other. Imagine the young happy child who gets up and has all sorts of fun enjoying new gifts and now he must rush to leave all of his stuff behind. As parents we want to spend every holiday with our children, but is it really their emotional highs we are concerned about, or our own? We need to let them be children.

If you use an alternating schedule rather than a shared-day schedule, the children can have one continuous holiday without interruptions and hassles. If it is your year to enjoy it with your children, it is all you. It may be better to thoroughly enjoy five of ten Christmases than to have ten broken and hassle-ridden ones. Additionally, children are less concerned with days of the week and dates of holidays. In some households Thanksgiving dinner is served on Wednesday or Friday, and in some neighborhoods Santa comes on December 26, right?

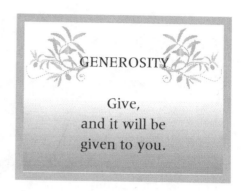

GENEROSITY

Give,
and it will be
given to you.

The first step in setting up a schedule that works best for your children is to come to an agreement as to what is a "holiday." There should be a set list. If it isn't listed, it isn't a holiday. If you want grandparents' day or the dog's birthday to be a holiday, you need to spell it out. Once you have your list of holidays, you should next define the parameters. For example:

> The Thanksgiving holiday will be defined as the period of time beginning at 6:00 p.m. on the night before Thanksgiving (a Wednesday) until 9:00 p.m. Thursday (Thanksgiving). In 2007, 2009, and all years ending in an odd digit, the Thanksgiving holiday will be spent with mom. In 2008, 2010, and all even years the Thanksgiving holiday (the same time period) will be spent with dad.

Scheduling vacation time can be done in a similar fashion. I have seen many written agreements and court orders that seem quite clear, only to be muddied up by parents who can't agree on anything. For example, let's suppose that the document states that each parent shall have the minor child for two weeks vacation during the summer. If dad usually only has little Johnny on every other weekend and on Wednesday nights, mom can wipe out a great deal of that father-son time by carefully selecting her "two weeks."

In such a scenario there are two periods in the month when dad goes six days without seeing his child (and more importantly, the child does not get to see his father). If mom "chooses" to start her "two weeks" after she has already had the child for her usual six-day uninterrupted stretch, she can now cause her two-

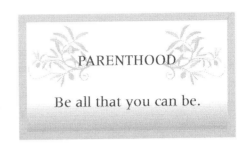

PARENTHOOD

Be all that you can be.

week vacation to last twenty straight days. For a father who feels that he already gets less time with his child than he should, this will not be acceptable.

If he were to respond in similar fashion when he takes his two-week vacation, he can turn it into seventeen straight days and the end result in each case is that the schedule is thrown out of whack and there can be a high degree of unpredictability throughout the summer. It can turn planning virtually everything else in the summer into a major headache for everyone. By the way, if you ask most people how many days there are in a week, what will they tell you?

One of the key elements that is necessary for any written agreement or court order regarding the allocation of holidays and vacations is to provide as much notice as possible and to provide a concrete and systematic method for providing notice where there are no specified times. Court orders or agreements commonly say that each parent is entitled to two weeks summer vacation. Even when parents do agree that two weeks equals fourteen days, there needs to be a mechanism for each parent to pick their two weeks of summer vacation so that the plans do not overlap and the schedules can be adjusted accordingly in a timely fashion.

One common method is to take an even-odd year approach to the first right of selection by stating, for example, in 2009 and all odd-numbered years, mom shall have the first selection of the two-week summer vacation (these weeks may be taken separately or consecutively) by April 1 of each year in writing, along with any known destination and itinerary information. Dad then has until May 1 to respond with his summer vacation plans for the year. In 2010 and all even-numbered years dad shall have the first selection of the two-

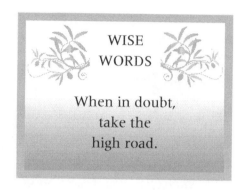

WISE WORDS

When in doubt, take the high road.

week summer vacation (these weeks may be taken separately or consecutively) by April 1 each year in writing along with any known destination and itinerary information. Mom then has until May 1 to respond with her summer vacation plans for the year.

One should also keep in mind that holidays and vacation times are generally special periods of time, and the parent who doesn't have the children should do their best not to interrupt such quality time. However, the parent who has the children should not be selfish and should still make efforts to ensure parent-child contact and communication.

Unfortunately, it is not uncommon for family law attorneys to receive phone calls on holidays or during periods of summer vacation because of poor planning or selfish parental interaction. I vividly remember one Christmas morning a few years ago when a hysterical client called me and then followed up with a lengthy e-mail because the children's mother had the audacity to call her ex-husband's house on Christmas morning at 11 a.m. to see how the children were enjoying the holiday since it was their father's turn to have them. The father and his new wife saw this act as an overt attempt to ruin *their* Christmas. The fact that my client and his new wife spent part of their Christmas morning calling me and writing me an e-mail to complain about the children's mother was absolutely astonishing.

If children in such circumstances are deprived of those special moments, one can only wonder how they feel throughout the rest of the year.

Holiday and Vacation Don'ts

- Don't attach demands and ultimatums to your response to any holiday or vacation requests from the other parent.
- Don't unilaterally make changes or make plans that would otherwise encroach on the other parent's scheduled time with the children.
- Don't call and pester the other parent during holiday or vacation time; you will have your time as well.
- Don't bother rehashing past scheduling problems.
- Don't make smart-ass or sarcastic comments about how you believe the other parent will spend his or her time with or without the children.
- Don't lay guilt trips on the children about missing them, leaving you, or anything like that.
- Don't ruin your children's holidays and vacations by arguing about them.

For some reason, many parents fail to provide itinerary or contact information when taking their children away for vacation. Here are some typical "reasons" for this lack of courtesy: "It is none of your business"; "He is with me, so don't worry about it"; "You have my cell number"; "You don't need the address or phone number, we'll call you if there is any emergency."

I once heard a well-respected judge put these issues into proper perspective. The mother of the child at issue in this particular ongoing saga asked why she should have to provide such information to the father when she took young Andrew on vacation, especially when his father never provided her with any such information? The judge's response was, "Ma'am, because that is what normal decent parents do!"

Be Decent

Coping with divorce can be especially difficult during the holidays. Sadness, anger, and

RELAX

Enjoy the little things and the big things take care of themselves.

regret may overwhelm you at a time that should be exciting and happy. Memories of happier times emphasize the unwelcome changes divorce brings. You may dread holiday get-togethers that you used to anticipate with pleasure. It's difficult enough to deal with your own emotions; facing family and friends is often too much to bear. Financial uncertainty may create worry where once you enjoyed being a generous giver.

For children, divorce turns the holidays upside down. They are torn, wanting to be with both parents. They worry that the holidays won't be the same. Will they see grandma? Will Santa find them? Will they get any presents? They hide their bigger fears about how divorce will change the family behind a litany of fears about holiday activities and traditions.

When it comes to holidays and vacations, it is helpful to remember that there are not enough of them in life. We need to take extra care and attention when we are separated and divorced to have our children enjoy as many holidays and vacations with each parent as possible. Don't rob your children of opportunities to spend memorable holidays and vacations with their other parent. Be decent. Proper planning and some mature and reasonable behavior can go a long way in accomplishing this goal.

Writing Letters & E-mail

S ometimes there's a good reason to write a letter or an e-mail to your ex. Regardless of the reason for writing, there are some helpful guidelines to follow. When you write to the other parent, for better or for worse, you are forever memorializing your words. You can't retract them, and your written words might come back to haunt you, so it's best to use restraint.

However, written communication can often be much more effective than verbal communication. It is usually easier to be polite and professional when writing because you have time to plan and think things through. Notice I said it is *usually* easier. Following the dos and don'ts will help you write effective and appropriate letters and e-mails.

Writing Dos

☞ Pretend the judge will read every word. Imagine he or she will judge you only on that letter.

- Be professional and businesslike; pretend you are writing to a colleague.
- Keep the communication child-focused.
- Have a benevolent purpose in mind before you write.

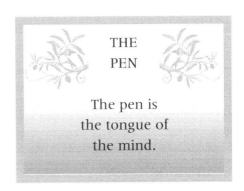

THE PEN

The pen is the tongue of the mind.

- Read, re-read, and re-read again, asking yourself if there is anything that you have written that can be misconstrued or might be subject to different interpretations.
- Request action.
- Don't forget to express gratitude or praise for something — anything. That kind of communication can go a long way.
- Reinforce positive behavior.

Writing Don'ts

- Don't assume anything. Communicate everything to make sure there's clarity.
- Don't make demands. Make *requests* — humbly.
- Avoid threats, criticism, name-calling, sarcasm, condescension, and blame. (Keep that judge in mind.)
- Don't rehash the past. Remember, there's supposed to be a child-focused purpose to this communication.
- Don't indicate that you will act unilaterally by a certain date or time if you get no further response. In other words, don't say something like this: "If I don't hear from you by 6:00 p.m. today, I will assume that you agree that I can keep Tyrone overnight tonight." WRONG!

The Mighty Pen

Becoming proficient in writing to the other parent is no easy task. It takes time, effort, and patience. It can also require a great deal of self-control. I have authored hundreds of letters and rough drafts of letters to my son's mother since we separated in 1994. I could show you numerous examples of good letters and, unfortunately, plenty of others that should never be emulated. I frequently assist clients in improving their written communication skills so that they can effectively accomplish their child-focused objectives when interacting with the other parent. If you have trouble discussing information about the children with the other parent, I suggest you work on mastering this important skill.

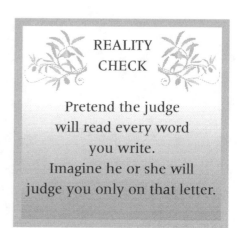

REALITY CHECK

Pretend the judge will read every word you write. Imagine he or she will judge you only on that letter.

Written communication can be so important in these situations that I'd like to go one step further. If you would like a free personal critique of any brief letter that you have sent or intend to send to your child's other parent, you may send it to me via e-mail and I will e-mail you my comments and suggestions. This is one small way that I can say thank you for reading. Visit my website, www.mikethelawyer.com, for more information on these services or send me an e-mail at mike@mikethelawyer.com and include "Mike, I read your book" in the subject line.

25

Unreasonable Denial of Visitation

When there is an ongoing power struggle over the amount of time that each parent wants to spend with the children, things can heat up quickly. Often one parent, usually the father, will not be "allowed" to spend time with the children as requested even when the other parent is not exercising parental time herself. For example, assume that dad has moved out and that he has a suitable home where the children can spend time with him. Further assume that the separation is relatively new and that there is no court order or written agreement concerning visitation in place yet.

Quite naturally, this hypothetical father has requested to spend as much time as possible with the children. He is a good dad and there is no bona fide reason that he should not be with his children as much as their mother is with them. Mom, unfortunately, is downright furious that her no-good husband actually made good on his threats to move out. He must be punished. His price to pay is that she will unilaterally and unreasonably deny his requests for time with the children. It happens all the time.

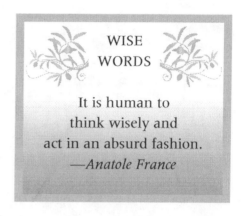

WISE
WORDS

It is human to
think wisely and
act in an absurd fashion.
—*Anatole France*

I am not aware of any studies that have attempted to quantify the number of reported domestic violence incidents relative to the denial of child access between separated and divorcing couples. However, based on the professional experiences of a great many family law practitioners, I firmly believe that a significantly large percentage of the most tumultuous arguments, physical altercations, or acts of domestic violence occur when someone is being jerked around out of spite — when all the person wants is to spend time with the children. In such circumstances the anger will often simmer to an uncontrollable boiling point.

If you're engaged in a power struggle over the kids, consider the following thoughts and suggestions.

- Assume that the children want a relationship with both parents. Understand they will avoid at all costs the appearance of disloyalty in the eyes of either parent.
- Children should not have to choose between parents. Do not put them in the position of having to show partiality.
- Do not expect to rapidly reform the behavior of the other parent. Be realistic. It helps to accept that this person may never change. Go about doing the best you can for your children, given the other parent's current character traits and disposition.

- Build goodwill if possible. Be quick to acknowledge reasonable behavior and cooperation when it occurs.

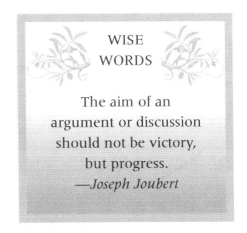

WISE WORDS

The aim of an argument or discussion should not be victory, but progress.
—*Joseph Joubert*

Not to be sexist here, but let's assume that it is primarily the dads who are not the primary custodians. I think that is a fact. Consequently, dads are more often the parent *requesting* to spend time with the children. For the men, I offer the following suggestions.

- Give as much reasonable notice as possible for your requests to spend time with your children.
- Manners count; name-calling and hanging up on people rarely helps.
- No one likes demands or ultimatums.
- Do not threaten to take custody or have her thrown in jail.
- Make it known that you wish to have the first option of spending time with the children before any baby-sitters or third parties are utilized.
- Don't keep asking when the answer is no; this is one of those times when no usually means no.
- Request that you be contacted if she should "reconsider."
- Suggest alternative dates and times if your initial request is denied.
- Keep a detailed communication log of all your interaction with your ex.
- If you are "allowed" time, use it wisely and build upon your relationship with your children.

- Avoid criticizing the other parent for not spending time with the children.
- Don't drink or use drugs when the children are with you. (This should go without saying, but there are a surprising number of cases involving drunk driving with the children in the car during visitation.)
- If you are offered any time with your children, no matter when, how limited, or how short the notice, do whatever you can to take it. (Your golf tee time should take a back seat).
- Keep your time with the children as your time with the children; it is not time to mix new relationships and other activities involving friends or new significant others (at least not for a while).
- Do not discuss requests for time in front of the children.

For the women, it may be helpful to consider the following:

- Dads are parents too.
- Children need parents, not just weekend visitors.
- Denying visitation is not fair to your children.
- It is simply wrong to use your children to "punish" your ex. They are not weapons.
- When children grow up, they often resent the parent who interfered with their relationship with the other parent.
- You could use a break; make good use of the time that the children are not with you.
- When it comes to financial matters, including child support, there is far more voluntary compliance when there is true reasonable and liberal access to the children and involvement in their lives.
- In a custody battle one of the biggest strikes against you could

be a judge believing that you (as the primary custodian) would jerk the father around, whereas he would not do the same to you.

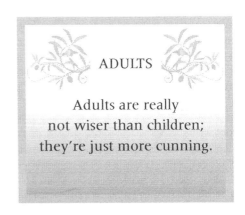

ADULTS

Adults are really not wiser than children; they're just more cunning.

- You are your own worst court witness when you get caught unreasonably denying visitation.

- Women do lose in court, more and more often.

Do not unreasonably deny parental time, access, and involvement to the other parent; just don't do it. When you are not able to spend time with the children, you should immediately offer the other parent the chance to do so. If they can't, or choose not to do so, you have done your part. In fact, regardless of all else going on, one of the best things that you can do to calm custody chaos is to go out of your way to demonstrate that denying visitation will not be part of your modus operandi. Take that potential allegation off the table as quickly as you can.

26

My Time vs. Your Time: Scheduling

When I first became a separated parent and realized that life would become much different than I imagined, I had a difficult time embracing the fact that I would have to parent by a specific and rigid schedule. The ongoing difficulties associated with having a child in common with someone you have great trouble dealing with can seem overwhelming at times. You may feel like you will be stuck in such a situation for years on end. In that situation, I have found it really helps if you adhere to a schedule and limit your requests to deviate from that schedule.

I think I can already hear your objections. You may feel the way I did — it shouldn't be this way. Perhaps. But it *is* this way. Trust me when I say that living by the schedule is better than not living by it. I definitely felt that my parenting time shouldn't have to be only on certain days of the week and certainly not only on every other weekend. What if there was something special and it didn't fall on "my weekend"? I thought that my baby's mamma and I should be able to adjust times, schedules, and events around our schedules. Surely, one would surmise, two reasonable adults can make schedule adjustments concerning their child's life, as needed, at any given time. Wow! Wouldn't that be nice?

I quickly found that many people experience the same

> **TOGETHERNESS**
>
> We sleep in separate rooms;
> we have dinner apart;
> we take separate vacations.
> We are doing everything
> we can to keep our
> marriage together.
> —*Rodney Dangerfield*

frustrations and that they, too, are disappointed when schedule adjustments don't work out. Unfortunately, it's common for newly separated parents to resist a set schedule. In the immediate aftermath of a breakup, especially if emotions are running high, scheduling issues can be a real disaster. In short, my personal and professional experience has demonstrated that the sooner you can get to a fair and reasonable schedule and stick to it, the less you will argue and fight over all child-related issues.

It really is best to limit the opportunities for disagreements. Following a set schedule will help immensely. If there is no agreed upon child access arrangement or no court-ordered schedule in place, parenting (and life in general) may become significantly more difficult.

Even when there is a schedule in place, frequent requests to modify the child access arrangements, especially early on, can lead to problems. So, fight the urge to make lots of scheduling adjustments. Parents will often keep score when it comes to deviating from the schedule; they will base their decision to honor a scheduling adjustment request on the way they have been treated when making similar requests. When that happens, the focus strays from benefiting the children to fixating on "tit for tat" discussions.

If a simple scheduling matter like taking your child to the circus causes problems, then it may not be worth the aggravation to suggest the changes. It is best to stick to the schedule and adjust your

COOL

Nothing gives one person so much advantage over another as to remain cool and unruffled under all circumstances.

life accordingly. These life adjustments are far better than constant arguing and fighting. Having to miss out on things is just another sacrifice to be made when parents decide not to stay together. If you do decide to request a change or a switch in the schedule, you should give as much notice as possible and state why you're suggesting the change. When you do so, state why the schedule change will benefit the children. It is not about accommodating you. That will generally not be persuasive.

To get out of keeping score, teach by example. If you can be big enough to "give in" to a schedule adjustment request, don't ask for make-up time. Try to get out of that habit. But, if scheduling accommodations are a virtual "one-way street," it may occasionally be necessary to hold your ground and not give in to make a point. However, keep in mind that one of your noblest child friendly goals should be to do all that you can to promote a give-and-take parenting relationship. Someone has to get it started. Remember the line from an old hymn, "Let peace begin with me"?

When there is a permanent schedule in place (keeping in mind that when it comes to child custody and visitation, everything is subject to future modification by the courts) and when the schedule is followed, life is significantly easier for everyone. It is often best to conduct yourself by acting as if you will only have your children on the days and times that are spelled out in your court order; without exception. Simply put — you can only schedule activities and do things with your children when those things fall during your "scheduled" time. This is not as bad as it sounds. In fact, it is beneficial in many respects.

To illustrate this point, I will share the basic 50-50 residential schedule (holiday and vacation times excluded for now) that has governed my life, my son's life, and my ex-wife's life for more than a decade. What it cost me to get there is another story for another day. After you grasp the schedule, I will point out some of the advantages and disadvantages of sticking to it.

Court Order

That the Plaintiff and Defendant shall have shared physical custody of the said minor child in accordance with the following schedule:

A. The minor child shall be in the care of the Plaintiff on Mondays and Tuesdays (overnights) and alternating Fridays, Saturdays, and Sundays (overnights) with the transition occurring after school (from school) during the school year, and at 6:00 p.m. during the summer and in the event that school is closed.

B. The minor child shall be in the care of the Defendant on Wednesdays and Thursdays (overnights) and alternating Fridays, Saturdays and Sundays (overnights) with the transition time occurring after school (from school) during the school year, and at 6:00 p.m. during the summer and in the event that school is closed.

C. The party exercising parental time with the minor child shall be responsible for returning the child to the other parent at 6:00 p.m. as outlined above. When the transitions occur after school, the receiving party shall be responsible for picking up the minor child from school.

The plain English translation is that the "said minor child" always spends the night with one parent on Mondays and Tuesdays and with the other on Wednesdays and Thursdays, and they alternate Friday, Saturday, and Sunday nights. It is a basic five-two and two-five set alternating schedule; the child spends five consecutive overnights with mom, followed by two overnights with dad, then two with mom and then five with dad.

If you have such a schedule, you don't have to spend time figuring out if it is your Monday or your Tuesday or her Wednesday, and so forth. In my case, if something falls on a Monday or Tuesday evening, I instantly know that my son is with me. If it is a Wednesday or Thursday night activity, I know that my son is with his mom.

Such a schedule seems fair. The benefits outweigh the drawbacks. Both parents can plan around it without constantly having to interact with each other over scheduling issues. Both parents will miss out on some things. Sometimes the schedule may benefit you, sometimes it won't. Like life in general, there are many times when things will go in your favor, and many times when they will not. Both you and your children will get over it.

Scheduling Dos

Focus on what you can do when the children are scheduled to be with you.

Recognize that the other parent is equally as blessed or cursed at times by adhering to a set schedule.

Try to be accommodating in changing things for the other parent to build "goodwill" for the future.

Recognize that if you get into the habit of making scheduling accommodations when asked, it will increase the odds that one day you will receive the same courtesies.

Teach by doing.

Lead by example.

> ### WISE WORDS
>
> No matter what you've done for yourself or for humanity, if you can't look back having given love and attention to your own family, what have you really accomplished?
> —*Lee Iacocca*

Scheduling Don'ts

Don't make plans with your children, or concerning your children, that do not fall on your scheduled time.

Don't let your children know about "tentative plans" that they will "miss out on" if the other parent won't adjust the schedule.

Don't set your children up for disappointment over scheduling change requests.

Don't dwell on things that you or your children miss because the schedule isn't in your favor.

If you find yourself in never-ending battles over who gets the kids on this day or that day, you need to hope that these scheduling fights will get "old" before the children do. The good news is that by the time your children hit the teenage years difficult parents do often lighten-up with each other. The bad news is that dealing with teenagers presents a whole new type of parent-child scheduling dilemma, so save your energy!

REALITY CHECK

Living by a schedule is a small price to pay to avoid never-ending scheduling turmoil. In fact, if you are in a moderate- to high-conflict parental tug of war over your children, you should embrace a fixed schedule like you would a trusted friend.

27

It Could Be Worse

No matter how bad things may seem, someone always has it worse. During child custody and visitation disputes it is especially helpful to put things into perspective. Too often in the busy and self-absorbed lifestyles of our times, we fail to slow down, reflect, and appreciate. Occasionally, it is healthy to stop, look, listen, and give thanks.

Unfortunately, it often takes something like an earthquake, tornado, or tsunami to connect us with our compassionate inner self. When going through separation and divorce, it is easy to feel sorry for yourself and to cloud the future by living in the past, blaming yourself, and otherwise feeling a sense of loss and ingratitude. During these times of despair, however, it is more important than ever to be a genuine and giving person. Keep your eyes and ears open for things to be grateful for and appreciate the many gifts that have been bestowed upon you.

You may not get to spend each day with your children, but at least you get to spend some days with them. Your schedule may not accommodate all the things you'd like to do with your children, but fortunately it will accommodate some of them. For many families, it is a major accomplishment to sit together at the dinner table for a meal, or to simply enjoy conversation in the fellowship of family.

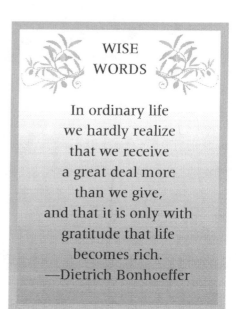

WISE WORDS

In ordinary life
we hardly realize
that we receive
a great deal more
than we give,
and that it is only with
gratitude that life
becomes rich.
—Dietrich Bonhoeffer

Going through a separation and divorce can easily bring out the worst in us. It's so easy to focus on your own problems when you have a lot of them. But do yourself and your children a favor by taking time to look at others, gain some perspective, and be thankful. You need to develop an appreciation for the intangibles of life. It helps — immensely.

Going through a divorce and embarking on the journey of single parenting is the time to dig deep. You will find what you are made of if the motivation is strong enough. The love between parent and children can indeed be one of the most powerful human motivators. Most people would do anything for their children. You are stronger than you think. No matter how bad it seems, you need to focus on what you have — the gifts that have been given to you and how fortunate you are to even have a child.

On my blog, www.DivorceWithoutDishonor.com/inspire, I share some brief stories, including stories about three special people and situations that reminded me that things could always be worse. The first reminder was the death of an old grade school friend.

Thirty-two-year-old husband and father of three, John E. Larkin, III, died in May of 1996 after a long and gallant battle with cancer. John carried his cross with courage and dignity and his faith and love for God never wavered. John was one of those people who could make you feel grateful for what you have without saying a word.

OPPORTUNE MOMENTS

Be on the lookout for any opportunities that can give you pause to think, to reflect, and to regroup.

The second significant situation, which happened in 1999, was the sudden illness — and resulting permanent blindness — that my son's former baseball coach, Colin Healy, experienced. The illness nearly killed him, and once again I was reminded of how fragile life is and how much we take for granted.

Another opportunity for reflection and thanks presented itself two years later when my son and I met eleven-year-old Mattie J. T. Stepanek, poet and peacemaker (July 17,1990 - June 22, 2004), at his first Baltimore book signing. These amazing people all have helped me to keep things in perspective and have inspired me by example.

Perhaps you currently feel as if you have little to be thankful for while you struggle to see light at the end of the tunnel. Start by being thankful for everything about your children. Regardless of your religious or philosophical beliefs, the birth of a child is nothing short of a miracle. A newborn is the ultimate gift to be nurtured, cared for, and cherished.

If you focus on what is most important today, then in the years ahead you will be able to look back and remember the special moments that you had with your children, even during all the chaos.

What is most important is the quality of the relationship with your children and spending as much time with them as possible. Your life is not a dry run. Make the most of the time you have. When times are tough, count your blessings and give thanks. It is a stop that you may need to take on the path to Big Rock. I was glad that I did.

REALITY CHECK

When you arise
in the morning,
give thanks for the
morning light,
for your life and strength;
give thanks for your life
and the joy of living.
If you see no reason
for giving thanks,
the fault lies
within yourself.

28 Children as Messengers & Spies

C hildren should rarely be asked to relay messages to their other parent. Asking a child to do so is yet another lose-lose proposition. By asking your child to be a messenger, you do nothing to improve your parental communication skills. Furthermore, you place your child in the middle of an area already ripe for a communication meltdown. Even a seemingly simple and benevolent message can lead to chaos.

Here's an example that may sound familiar: "Tell your father that we have plans on Friday night so he can pick you up on Saturday at 10 a.m., instead of Friday at 6 p.m." In a case like this, mom may be pretending, or even genuinely believing, that she is doing a good deed by giving dad advance notice and avoiding any confrontation between the two of them over this issue. Either way, she is WRONG!

Let's look at the potential pitfalls in this one simple scenario:

- The child forgets (or because of the desire to avoid conflict, pretends to forget), and the result is that dad shows up on Friday night and no one is home.

> **THE TRUTH**
>
> Actions speak louder than words, and they tell fewer lies.

- The child tells dad as instructed by mother and dad blows a fuse. The result is a bad transition time for father and child.
- Dad says, "When you go back to your mother, tell her that I will be there as scheduled," and the child forgets (or pretends to forget) to deliver the message.
- The child feels apprehensive, doesn't want to hurt dad's feelings, and is upset with mom for "causing" this dilemma.
- Dad says, "Tell your mom that you better be there on Friday night as planned or I'll _____ (call the police, call my lawyer, file contempt proceedings)."
- It's Friday night, mother wants child to go to the planned event, and the child is apprehensive about that because of the situation; child is expecting dad to show up and cause a scene.
- The next morning is a bad exchange in front of the child if any such scenarios actually took place.
- When dad arrives on Saturday, the child may get the third degree about what plans were "so important." Bad-mouthing mom then becomes more likely.
- Questions like what, where, when, and why (and, who was there?) may potentially consume the initial transition.
- What if dad had special plans for Friday night that the child would have really enjoyed?

All of this can be avoided when parents act like grown-ups and do their own communicating. There is almost never a reason for your children to act as go-betweens. It can be avoided with a little effort and some creative maneuvering. When you allow yourself to use your children

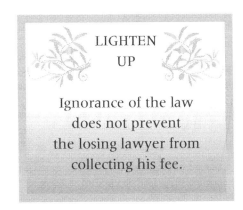

LIGHTEN
UP

Ignorance of the law
does not prevent
the losing lawyer from
collecting his fee.

as messengers, you're really placing responsibility on them that belongs to you. Don't load your children down with your own burdens. Don't make life easier for yourself by making it more complicated for them.

If treating your children as messengers isn't bad enough, it is really inappropriate to treat them like spies. When they are told to report on the activities of the other parent, it places the children in a no-win situation. Even worse, using your children as spies has some other negative consequences. It promotes lies and deceit. It promotes picking sides. And, it creates loyalty conflicts for the children. As a result, children may clam up or become untruthful or untrustworthy.

It can be difficult to break the habit of inappropriately questioning your children after they return from time with the other parent, but it must be done. A little child-focused thinking should get you there. Think about how it feels for your children to transition from one home to the other. When they return to you, they want to know you're happy to see them and that you're focused on them. Interrogation does not start "your" time off on a good note, and it makes children very uncomfortable whether they outwardly show it or not. Furthermore, if your children are worried that they'll have to "report" to you, transition time will be awkward for them. Instead of focusing on how your children already spent their time, focus on *how you're going to spend* your time with them.

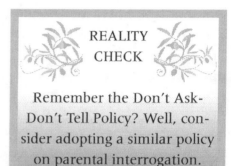

REALITY CHECK

Remember the Don't Ask-Don't Tell Policy? Well, consider adopting a similar policy on parental interrogation.

Obviously, there are some common-sense exceptions. Real and legitimate safety or health issues fall into that category. But that's not what I'm talking about here. I'm talking about when you want to know whether daddy's new girlfriend went to the zoo with them. Don't make such a situation even more unpleasant for your children. They'll tell you what they want to tell you, and they'll be a whole lot more likely to do so when you don't give them the third degree.

Children are smarter than you think. Simple communication designed to surreptitiously interrogate the children is not going to work for long. They will try desperately to exercise their right to remain silent. The reason they will do this is because they know that anything they say can and will generally be used against them — in one way or another! Again, the key is to focus on the life you and your children live together.

29
Perceptions, Truth & Deceptions

In child custody cases, too much emphasis is placed on challenging the truth about inconsequential parental allegations and defenses. For example, if dad was fired for stealing from an employer before the children were even born, it may still seem damaging to his credibility — especially if he gets caught lying about it. But this type of coup de grace will not win a custody battle. When one parent uses baby-sitters instead of offering the children to the other parent, this too may not be of any significance to the judge (even if the parent has lied about it and since been shown to have lied). Similarly, no one will be overly excited about allegations of constant tardiness at transition times.

Dueling parents usually overlook the fact that it is *how* and *to what degree* things *affect their children* that has the greatest impact upon a judge's decision in awarding custody. Child custody litigants are often frustrated when the other side has clearly been caught in certain lies and the judge seems to overlook or ignore them. Indeed, some categories of lies will never determine the final outcome of a highly contested child custody case. However, there are certain kinds of falsehoods that not only damage one's case, but most certainly negatively im-

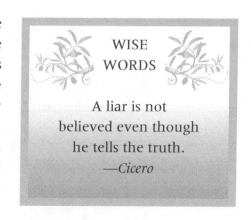

WISE
WORDS

A liar is not
believed even though
he tells the truth.
—*Cicero*

pact children of separated or divorcing parents. They are lies to, about, from, and involving the children.

Often in contested custody cases, parents and children are required to be "evaluated" and reports are made and submitted to the court. One of the more difficult and potentially damaging areas of child custody litigation occurs when the case involves mental health evaluations and clinical interviews. These evaluations and clinical interviews can take on many forms and serve a variety of purposes for the finder of fact. When child custody litigants and their children are required to submit to court-ordered evaluations, a whole new quagmire of complex problems can result.

An evaluator may be called as a witness to testify about their "findings" and their opinions based on information they have obtained from the parties or their respective allies and the children. It is in this context that lies can have a significant impact. Evaluators and mental health providers may also be called upon to offer their opinion on relevant hypothetical questions from the attorneys or the presiding judge. When the findings and opinions of the "experts" are flawed because of false information, the rules of reason and logic may lead to the wrong conclusions.

Remember, it is the judge who is supposed to sift through all the conflicting testimony and weigh all the factors as to what is ultimately his or her "best guess" regarding what is in the child's best interests. When the truth goes undetected in these situations in particular, a great deal of damage can be done. When information used by court-appointed evaluators is obtained from (or intentionally omitted by) parents and children who do not tell the

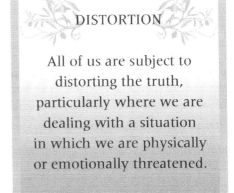

DISTORTION

All of us are subject to distorting the truth, particularly where we are dealing with a situation in which we are physically or emotionally threatened.

truth, the children's best interest may not truly be served.

We all know that children are easily influenced, manipulated, and otherwise susceptible to adult suggestiveness. In fact, adults can influence the "memories" of children even when they do not intend to. Additionally, a child's perception and an adult's perception of identical events can be entirely different. I once read a small article in a lawyer's journal that aptly illustrates the point. The article described a case involving a man charged with a murder witnessed by his four-year-old foster child. The child testified in court and told the jury how he saw the accused hit the victim repeatedly while she was on the ground and that his foster father had put something over the deceased's mouth. The defense attorney did not challenge what the child saw, but instead he had a forensic child psychiatrist explain to the jury that because of the way children's minds develop, young children are extremely literal. The expert witness went on to explain that, at four years of age, this particular child witness had perhaps accurately described what he saw, but from a child's perspective.

Later in the trial, the criminal defense attorney presented the jury with a 911 tape in which the dispatcher was giving the accused

CPR instructions. The instructions were consistent with what the defendant actually did and what the child actually saw on the night of the alleged murder. What the child testified to seeing and what the dispatcher instructed the accused to do on the tape was virtually identical. When the defendant found the victim unconscious on the floor, he called 911, left the phone on the table, and hit the speakerphone button. While receiving instructions from the 911 operator, this innocent foster father rolled the "victim" over, patted her on her back, then attempted to clear the airway with a rag and thereafter began pushing on her chest and continued with CPR efforts.

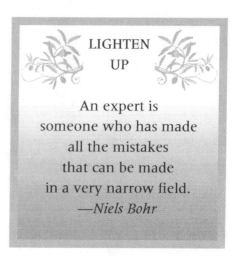

LIGHTEN UP

An expert is someone who has made all the mistakes that can be made in a very narrow field.
—*Niels Bohr*

Is there any question that children and adults can use different words to describe the same events? This works the other way too. Even though it is hard to distinguish a child's perception from a child's deception, the problem is compounded in clinical custody evaluations when the parents deliberately lie or misinform the experts. Unfortunately, this is a common problem.

Over the years I have collected volumes of information and articles on numerous child custody issues. I have spoken to many people who bring all sorts of opinions, backgrounds, and expertise to the equation.

When Parents Lie in Child Custody Cases — Leon A. Rosenberg, Ph.D.

In the 1990s I communicated with a veteran clinical psychologist, Leon A. Rosenberg, Ph.D., from the world-renowned Johns Hopkins

Hospital in Baltimore, Maryland. Several years later I came across an article written by Dr. Rosenberg and I kept that too. While pulling many of my sources together in writing this book, I tracked down Dr. Rosenberg after his retirement from thirty-seven years on the Hopkins faculty. It is with his permission that I will provide you with one of his works:

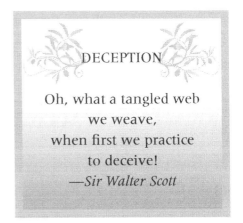

DECEPTION

Oh, what a tangled web
we weave,
when first we practice
to deceive!
—*Sir Walter Scott*

When a parent is struggling with a custody visitation battle and is forced to submit to an evaluation by a mental health specialist, the parent certainly wants to present well. You should not expect a parent to be totally open and honest. You expect them to exaggerate what they see as their best points and avoid or gloss over deficiencies. But when they have done something they feel can seriously be held against them, they may lie. I have had three recent cases where parents have lied to me about their personal (i.e., romantic) relationships with new partners, occurring after separation from their spouses. From each parent's point of view the results were disastrous. Not because I "caught" them lying. On the contrary, I was completely fooled. The other side, however, managed through their investigations to admit evidence that these relationships existed, which allowed the attorneys to present a hypothetical to me during my testimony, the answers to which were potentially quite harmful to these parents' cases.

All three cases had much in common. My child custody assessment in each case was by court order. The parents had been separated from their spouses for some time. They each had a young child in the home between the ages of four and six. One parent also had a two-year-old. No one was behaving inappropriately in the presence of the children. Sexual activities were carried out in private. One parent had the new partner sleep over occasionally and the child saw them together having breakfast. Another child was aware that mother and mother's friend shared a bed. The child saw them there in the morning. The children always saw the adults fully clothed. And in each case there was only one new partner. Holding hands, brief hugs, and good-bye kisses were the only physical contacts seen by the children.

Of major importance was the fact that all three parents had encouraged their children to keep the relationship secret and not talk about the "new friend" when they were with the other parent. In two cases, the relationship started after the separation. In one case, the relationship started before the separation and the child had met the person when she and her parent took trips to the zoo. The child was to keep this observation secret from the other parent.

I have seen many children in this type of evaluation and I certainly have had children tell me about secrets they have with mom or dad. Basically, most young children are not very skilled at keeping secrets. But a few apparently are and these children said nothing to suggest that they were involved in the deception. Indirect assessment of the children through projective drawings and storytelling did not yield anything to raise suspicion. Each parent lied to me when asked directly about this aspect of their life. In two of the cases, allegations had been made that the parent had a relationship with another person that had started after the separation. At the time of my involvement, these remained unsubstantiated allegations. All three parents told me that they were rarely dating, that the children were never involved, and they did not have an ongoing relationship with anyone.

Hence, I appeared in court ignorant of this important aspect of their lives. And what I believe is most important, I did not have the opportunity to examine what, if any, impact these relationships might have had on the children. The omission was quite important.

In each case the other parent's lawyer presented me with a hypothetical where I was to assume that a parent had a relationship with a person other than the spouse and had instructed the child to keep it a secret. What was the potential impact on the child? The hypotheticals presented different details, but essentially followed the above format, and I was forced to describe the well-known negative impact on children exposed to such parental conflict and deception. Typically children are struggling with loyalty conflicts when dealing with divorce and the last thing they need is to be involved in some deceptive practice by one of the parents where the child is required to demonstrate greater loyalty to one parent over the other.

The only answer that can be given to such a hypothetical is a generalization from clinical experience and, to some degree, from reports in the professional literature. Even after pointing out that not every child responds negatively, and that every situation has its unique features that might make the outcome different, the general finding is a negative outcome, usually in terms of symptoms of anxiety in the child.

What if I had been told the truth in the first place? When this has happened in other cases, I have had a meeting with the child and the parent where the parent explains that I already know the truth, that the parent has told me all about it, and that there is nothing that the child has to keep secret from me. Then my evaluation of the child proceeds.

Certainly, the evaluation may turn out to be damaging to the parent. I may find that the child's emotional difficulties are being made worse by the secrecy issue. However, I may also find that a child is minimally discomforted by the secrecy game and in terms of all measures of emotional adjustment, no harm has been done. The child is doing well in school, maintains friendships, shows no sleeping, eating, or toileting difficulties, no regressive behavior, etc. This type of assessment outcome is certainly possible.

I try to deal with hypotheticals as carefully as possible. I insist on specifying that information missing in the hypothetical would be necessary in order to come to an answer, and if there is too much missing information, I explain why the lack of that information makes it impossible to answer the hypothetical. I explain that such answers are generalizations that, although basically true, may not be valid for specific cases. But a question that basically deals with an attack on the child's loyalty to one of the parents has to be answered because the knowledge base clearly indicates a significant risk of a negative outcome. To simply refuse to answer the hypothetical is not a viable option. To do so could suggest bias (i.e., you are protecting one parent).

Do parents understand this issue? I try to explain, in general terms, that it would be best if I could address all possible issues in my evaluation. But as already stated, people do lie when they feel they have to protect themselves. It is certainly understandable that a parent may view my role with some anxiety. But when — after the fact — I have discussed the problem with some parents, I have been left with the impression that they believed that the worst that could happen would be that my evaluation would be weakened or perhaps discredited by my ignorance of the true facts. They were not aware of the impact of the "fact" being brought into court. Perhaps this is an issue requiring better education of clients by their attorneys.

Dr. Rosenberg is a psychologist who is a member of the Johns Hopkins University School of Medicine faculty in the Division of Child and Adolescent Psychiatry. During his full-time tenure of thirty-eight years at the medical school and hospital, he examined and treated hundreds of victims of sexual abuse and also worked with children and adolescents suffering from other forms of trauma, as well as many types of mental illness. Since July of 2000 he has limited his work to child custody issues, child sexual abuse assessments, issues of mental illness diagnosis, and effects of trauma on children and adolescents, as well as other issues involving expertise in child and adolescent development and mental health.

The Bottom Line

Doctor Rosenberg concludes that when lies involve the perceptions of those caught in the middle or when parents place their children in the throes of their own deceptive practices, making the correct decision becomes a more difficult task for the trier of fact. When parents lie and involve their children, they usually do so at the expense of their children's psychological well-being. Telling the truth may not always be easy and certainly the truth may not always bring the outcome you hope for in your custody case, but your children's well-being rests in your hands. Telling the truth is another great way to be the superior parent.

30

Daycare Dilemmas

There are only so many hours in a day. You need to work to support yourself and your children (and probably to pay your lawyer). Life is hectic in the age of the new millennium and that is not likely to change in our lifetimes. So, depending on the age of your children, daycare and/or before and after school care is often an issue.

For parents in turmoil, childcare issues can be quite problematic. Even the baby-sitters and childcare providers are not immune. They are often part of the collateral damage in parental skirmishes. Third party caregivers already have great responsibilities tending to the needs of the children entrusted to them and in conforming to state and county regulatory laws and guidelines. They, like most third parties, do not like to have parental discord and transitional (pick-up and drop-off) issues thrust upon them.

Let's take a look at some of the numerous questions and

dilemmas that can arise from the simple need for daycare:

YOUR LEAD

Children are natural mimics who act like their parents in spite of every effort to teach them good manners.

☞ *Who?*
- Who will watch our child?
- Who will be allowed to pick up and drop off and who will not?
- Who is in charge of this place?
- Who is going to pay for this?

☞ *What?*
- What about using my mother, sister, or my brother's neighbor's second cousin as a baby-sitter?
- What terms, conditions, and ultimatums will be attached to any daycare proposals?
- What gives you the right to say who will watch our child?

☞ When?
- When do "we" need daycare?
- When can I pick up and drop off?
- When our child is with me, I am not using *your* daycare.

☞ Where?
- Where is this place?
- Where does it say that I can or cannot pick up my child from here?
- Where will you be while he/she is in daycare?

⫷ Why?
- Why do we need daycare?
- Why can't I watch him when you work or are unavailable and vice-versa?
- Why can't we just pick a place half-way between us?
- Why do you think this place is better than that place?
- Why can't I just show up there?

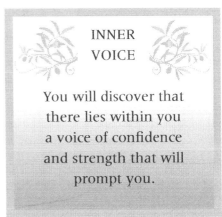

INNER VOICE

You will discover that there lies within you a voice of confidence and strength that will prompt you.

Sadly, all of these power struggles are so familiar to me that I will share a story from my own experience. I'm trying not to share too many in the course of this book because many could be offensive or embarrassing to some of the participants (including me). However, I feel compelled to share some of my past daycare issues to illustrate the absurdity of it all and to help prevent you from taking actions that are not in your children's best interests.

When my ex-wife and I separated, my son was not quite two years old. I was promised a 50-50 relationship prior to moving out. Upon separation that changed to "you will see him when I tell you that you can see him" and "the most you will get is one night a week and every other weekend." My response was, "Wrong!" and "I'll bury you before that ever happens." You see, I, too, had plenty of room to improve upon my interpersonal parental communication skills.

We were each self-employed and we both worked many and varied hours. We were each able to afford daycare and we each had a parent or family member(s) nearby that could help with daycare.

We lived twenty-five to thirty minutes apart. We could not agree on anything, much less daycare. We were destined for a nasty custody battle. The problem was that while the case was pending, no one technically had any more or less *legal* authority to do anything with respect to child rearing, absent a court order. Court orders take time to acquire and they too can be problematic. Like many newly separated couples, we were simply left to our own power struggles over who would be watching our son during the day.

With no schedule in place, it was pure hell. When we were provided an emergency schedule by the court (and that's *another* story), there was no temporary granting of legal custody as that issue would be decided "later." With all the court delays, the daycare dilemma evolved into a preschool problem. On days when my son was with me I used the YMCA daycare facilities. It was an excellent program and atmosphere. I paid for full-time use and offered the days that our son was with his mother to her for her use if, when, and as needed. She was furious and threatened to sue the YMCA because they did not have her permission for *her* son to go there.

At first, on days when our son was with his mother, she would use her mother, brother, and employees as sitters. I had a host of objections to those choices, especially given all of the family turmoil and lack of trust on all sides. One of my biggest fears early on, when we were both jockeying for position to lay claim to sole legal and physical custody, was that she would allege that she had decided to be a full-time stay-at-home mom. She could have easily afforded to do that and it would have made the initial need for daycare moot. I knew that if the picture were painted like that, it would make my battle for at least 50-50 all the more difficult.

Driven by both fear of the system and the love for my son, I decided to try to level the playing field in case the "stay-at-home mom" card was played. I contacted the State Child Care Administration and filled out the applications to become a licensed in-home daycare provider. I took all the classes and seminars, completed the background checks, provided the references, and arranged the interviews. I had my home modified; I made it child friendly inside and out, and I had all of the health and fire inspections completed. I purchased the cots and was granted a license to care for up to eight children.

In terms of jockeying for position, I now had a back-up plan. I would not only be a stay-at-home dad, but certified and state-approved as a childcare provider — with an emphasis on early childhood development. I saw no down side. By taking all of the courses, it kept my mind active and focused on positive things; my house was safe and child friendly and, to boot, I could provide my son with an environment filled with other children to enhance his social skills. It also showed that I was serious about my desire to spend as much time with my child as possible. The downside was that a judge might think I was a nut for putting my law practice on hold to watch toddlers during the day. I would take that risk, and I have learned since then that in some respects, representing divorce clients and parents in custody battles is not much different from running a daycare.

By the time all of the red tape was completed and I was granted my daycare license, the YMCA had become a real place of stability, enjoyment, and growth for my son. I decided that I was not going to disrupt his stability and progress by implementing my back-up plan. In hindsight, I have no doubt that it would have been a wonderful experience to run a daddy daycare, but in the end it was not supposed to be about what was best for me and my personal case-building efforts.

As our divorce case continued to meander through the court system, the daycare issues would resurface again and again. Eventually we were court-ordered to attend "clinical interviews" with a child psychologist to ascertain whether or not we were appropriate candidates for any form of joint custody. Although an immediate "no" should have been readily apparent, the process involved many individual sessions and meetings with both of us together with the good doctor, and meetings where we would each bring

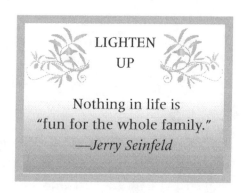

LIGHTEN UP

Nothing in life is "fun for the whole family." —*Jerry Seinfeld*

our son to be "observed" as to our respective parental interaction. Additionally, the doctor would evaluate and assess our son's bond and relationship with each of us.

By the time we had been court-ordered for this exercise in futility, the YMCA had obtained a new director and the legal department had to get involved because of the threatened lawsuit. I saw the writing on the wall that my son, because of his mother's interference (as I perceived it), would essentially get "kicked out" of preschool. As part of her "plan" to assert control over the daycare situation, she enrolled him in a completely different daycare/preschool program and used that center on *her* days. For our son: a new set of children, different routines, different nap times and activities, different providers, more confusion, greater disruption. It broke my heart when I read his progress report from there because it was obvious to me that attending two different preschools was not only patently absurd, it was devoid of any benefit to him. However, if we were no longer welcomed at the YMCA, then his mother's selection of a location near her home would be hard for me to argue against, regardless of how it came to be.

Given the timeliness of this daycare/preschool crisis, the child psychologist, who was also acting like a mediator in some respects, wanted us to tackle this issue and build upon that success and settle the case. It was clear that he fancied himself a gifted peacemaker and in the end I firmly believed that he did not care what we agreed to as long as he could say that he helped us reach "an agreement." Suffice it to say that after nearly twenty sessions and thousands of dollars, there was no agreement on our first and only issue — where our son should go to preschool.

Trust me; you don't want to walk our path. How can you avoid some common daycare dilemmas? Let's look at some dos and don'ts.

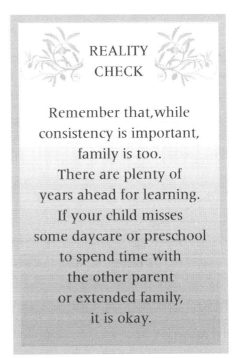

REALITY CHECK

Remember that, while consistency is important, family is too. There are plenty of years ahead for learning. If your child misses some daycare or preschool to spend time with the other parent or extended family, it is okay.

Daycare Dos

- Make sure that the provider is aware of any issues associated with the use of their services so that *they* can try to alleviate the other parent's concerns in a productive manner. More than likely, the other parent won't listen to what you have to say.

- Make sure that all people who may be picking up or dropping off your children are properly registered with the provider.

- Provide the daycare provider with a copy of any governing court order(s).

- Try as hard as you can to reach an agreement on who will be providing daycare and when and where.

- Try to limit the number of different daycare providers or baby-sitters.

- Remember that while consistency is important, family is too. There are plenty of years ahead for learning. If your child misses some daycare or preschool to spend time with the other parent or extended family, it is okay.
- Try to meet and interview the provider together if it is someone unknown to one or both of you.
- Make sure that all financial arrangements are made, and, if possible, make sure that only one person is actually paying the provider. (You can exchange money between yourselves; the provider should only have to deal with one person for billing issues.)
- Get the assistance of a mediator or neutral third party to help the two of you come up with child-focused solutions.

Daycare Don'ts

- Don't make unilateral decisions or enroll your child without at least making good faith attempts to discuss and agree on a specific provider.
- Don't get daycare providers involved in your parental disputes.
- Don't threaten to sue them.
- Don't disrupt their place of business.
- Don't attempt to restrict the other parent's access or involvement at the daycare.
- Don't discuss your personal problems with people at daycare.
- Don't have adult conversations in front of your child or in front of anyone else's child.

The Time Is Now

If you and your baby's other parent cannot agree on daycare- and preschool-related matters and if there are ongoing parental access disputes involving daycare or preschool, you need to go to great lengths to resolve these issues in a timely and amicable fashion. Trust me on this too; it will only get worse if the power struggle is not resolved when your children are young. If you can't agree on the need for, the location of, or the parameters of daycare or pre-school, you will have a long and difficult path to travel. The time to get on the right path is now.

School
Issues

When eight-year-old Gina received her school progress report, her father was the last to know. It came "home" with Gina, and Gina's mother never shared it or its contents with Gina's dad. Gina's mom, Maria, signed the progress report, turned it in, and requested a parent-teacher conference. Maria never told her ex-husband anything about the request for a parent-teacher conference.

When Maria came to the meeting, she brought her boyfriend, Walter, and introduced him to Mrs. Beasley as her fiancé. Maria then spent most of the conversation telling Mrs. Beasley about how Gina's dad, Tony, was really not that involved with Gina and that he was too concerned with himself to get involved in Gina's educational needs. She was quick to mention that she has sole custody and that Gina's father sees her every other weekend and on Wednesday evenings, "when he feels like it." At every opportunity during the meeting, Maria attempted to make herself look good while belittling Tony.

Not surprisingly, Maria neglected to tell Mrs. Beasley that Tony had unsuccessfully fought for custody of Gina and that he begs to see her on a weekly basis. She also forgot to mention that Gina ab-

WISE WORDS

Children are likely to
live up to
what you believe of them.
—*Lady Bird Johnson*

solutely adores her dad. Mrs. Beasley had no idea that Maria will not allow Tony any contact with his daughter other than what the court order provides. Even that is often subject to Maria's unilateral discretion.

When Tony found out about the progress report and the conference that he was never invited to attend, he was furious. He demanded that the teacher and principal meet with him immediately. Gina's dad wanted to know why he'd never received the progress report and why he wasn't informed about the meeting. He also wanted to know if "that redneck" had been there too. He wanted to know what "they" said about *him*. At the meeting, Tony spent the majority of his time telling Mrs. Beasley about what a terrible mother Gina was and how she excludes him from everything. He wanted to show her letters and e-mails from Maria as well as copies of deposition transcripts proving what a liar Maria was when it came to him and his daughter.

Needless to say, Mrs. Beasley was left with a very negative impression of Gina's parents. Neither parent seemed cognizant of how foolish they looked. Neither seemed aware of the negative effects that their interaction would have on their child. As a result of all this nonsense, Gina was labeled. She came to be known as the adorable brown-eyed girl with the two dysfunctional parents.

Similar inclusion-exclusion power struggles play out in schools everywhere. And, sadly enough, there is no apparent end to the list of things that can be squabbled over:

- The sharing (or lack thereof) of information, papers, report cards, awards, projects, school pictures, and yearbooks
- The completion of emergency contact information cards and required school forms
- Permission slips
- Involvement of stepparents, grandparents, and significant others
- Parent-teacher meetings
- Selection of parent roles (primarily with younger children), such as parent helper, parent coordinator, class mom or dad, and the like
- Homework issues and forgetting things or leaving things at the other parent's house
- School uniforms and school clothes
- Messenger issues, such as relaying information to and through school officials to the other parent
- School sports, field trips, and extracurricular activities

When one parent seeks to exclude the other from such important matters in their children's lives, the other parent often feels that he is forced to fight yet another child custody and visitation battle just to be recognized. The formula is ripe for ongoing consternation. Ultimately, by being placed in the middle of all the parental dysfunction that circulates around the school setting, the children suffer and lose out. With little peace between homes and in school, children are profoundly and negatively impacted. Fortunately, there are ways to effectively deal with all of these issues so that no one is excluded and the children feel as if both parents are supportive of their school life.

School Dos

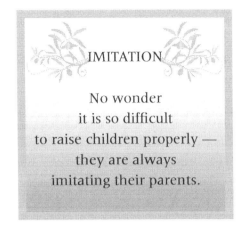

IMITATION

No wonder
it is so difficult
to raise children properly —
they are always
imitating their parents.

☞ Make sure that you provide the other parent with either an original or copy of every important paper that comes home from school.

☞ Provide your ex with a copy of any letters that you send to your children's teachers or school administrators.

☞ Use that copy machine, fax machine, and/or scanner that I mentioned earlier for the purpose of sharing information in a timely fashion.

☞ Use e-mail or make a family/school blog to post important events and information pertaining to school-related matters.

☞ If there is a custody order in place, make sure that the school has a copy of it on file.

☞ If you are the sole legal custodian of the children and your court order does not specify the rights of the other parent, notify the school in writing that you authorize them to provide any and all school-related information to the other parent.

☞ Whenever there is a place for the other parent's contact information, either provide it or give the other parent an opportunity to complete and return the form.

☞ If there are serious communication problems between you and the other parent, let the school know that there may be a need to be particularly alert to the dissemination of information pertaining to your children.

☞ Unless you think that you cannot control yourself in an appropriate fashion, try to schedule teacher meetings and parent conferences together with the other parent.

☞ Make a concerted effort to demonstrate a united front on as many issues as you can.

☞ If there are certain areas that can be delegated to a particular parent, do so, and share all information. For example, if one parent is an engineer and loves math, perhaps that parent could be the "math and science" parent and the other could focus on areas of his or her interest and ability.

School Don'ts

☞ Don't bad-mouth or belittle the other parent to teachers, staff, other parents, or children.

☞ Don't withhold information from the other parent.

☞ Don't encourage teachers or staff to withhold information from the other parent.

☞ Don't sign up for activities without presenting the other parent with the opportunity to do the same.

☞ Don't ask parents, teachers, or staff to "spy on" the other parent's interaction with the school personnel or other parents.

If You're Excluded

If the other parent has been given an opportunity to "play fair" and he or she has no interest or intention of following any of these suggestions, then you need to assert yourself in a positive fashion so as not to be excluded from your children's education. However, you must take great care not to inflame the situation. One option is to set up a meeting with your children's teachers and school administrators to explain to them that you feel as if you have been, or will likely be, excluded from receiving information and excluded from activities.

Let them know you want to be fully involved in your children's education and up-bringing and that you need their assistance. They are accustomed to seeing children caught in the middle of parents who do not communicate well. Be careful not to cast blame or speak ill of the other parent. Simply explain that

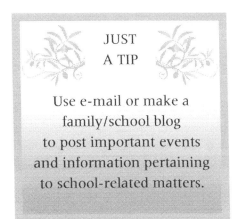

JUST
A TIP

Use e-mail or make a family/school blog to post important events and information pertaining to school-related matters.

there are communication issues and while you do not want to involve the school, you do want them to be aware of the situation. Explain that your only concern is the well-being of your children and that you want to know what is going on at school. Offer to provide self-addressed stamped envelopes of varied sizes and request that copies of all important documents and information be sent to you. Make sure that all of your contact information is on file. Ask for any suggestions and let them see that you are solution-oriented and that you are genuinely concerned about your children.

If you conduct yourself in a child-focused yet humble and respectful fashion, you will be pleased at how well you will likely be received by school officials. Like judges presiding over child custody cases, teachers hate to see children being used as weapons by one parent against the other.

Field Trips

When separated or divorced parents of preschool and elementary school children want to attend their child's school field trip, there can be trouble deciding which parent should go, or whether both should. If it is obvious that mom and dad should not be anywhere within eyesight (with or without binoculars) of one another, then there is the issue of who gets to go. If both parents insist on going, field trips cause a great deal of added stress for all participants, especially for the child. The good news is that by the time children reach puberty, they generally don't want either parent to go on a school field trip. To allow that to happen is just "un-cool."

In general, if a parent has the ability to attend field trips, it is often found to be a rewarding experience and a potential source of fond memories for years down the road. Children grow up so fast and before we know it, they are no longer so cute, cuddly, and innocent. The preschool and elementary school years may actually be the golden years of parenting. If both parents can participate and allow the field trip to be a pleasant and comfortable experience for the child, it can be especially soothing for child and parents alike — a sign that things will be okay. A successful field trip with both parents in atten-

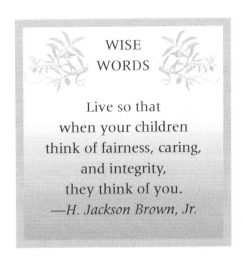

WISE WORDS

Live so that
when your children
think of fairness, caring,
and integrity,
they think of you.
—*H. Jackson Brown, Jr.*

dance can also go a long way in easing some of the inherent parental pain and guilt associated with having your child grow up with parents that live separate and apart.

If however, things heat up between parents on a school field trip, it can be a recipe for disaster. At a minimum, it will be a major embarrassment for the child and a source of parking lot gossip. If the parents are currently engaged in litigation and there is the uncertainty of a custody determination looming ahead, the problems are magnified. In preparing for court it is necessary to demonstrate that one has the makeup of that perfect parent. Surely, each litigant must attend school field trips, maybe even chaperone. A good lawyer, after all, wants third party witnesses, like other parents and teachers, to praise your parenting. Your family and friends are expected to say nice things. It is these disinterested third party witnesses that courts often want to hear from. But even without pending litigation, joint field trips are rarely in your child's best interest.

Here's a typical scenario. There is a field trip to a local pumpkin farm in October and your first grader is excited about it. Both parents would genuinely love to go and each has the ability to do so. There is custody litigation pending as well as moderate conflict in general, which sometimes reaches code-orange level. The field trip falls on a Wednesday and dad usually has little Billy on Wednesdays at 5:00 p.m. when he picks him up at the school after care program.

Last year, mom went on the kindergarten trip to the zoo. According to dad, mom didn't tell him in advance and

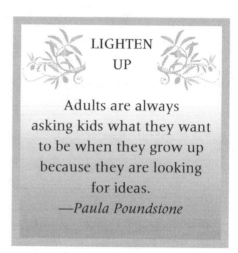

LIGHTEN UP

Adults are always asking kids what they want to be when they grow up because they are looking for ideas.
—*Paula Poundstone*

he had to miss it. According to mom, she did tell him, but he never listened. Mom further asserts that dad wouldn't have attended anyway because he never chose to participate in *anything* related to Billy's school activities. Dad acknowledges that last year he was away on business and he had to miss the trip to the zoo, but he is still angry because she did not know that he had to be out of town. And besides, if she would have given him a copy of the notice that came to her house, he could have rearranged his trip. Each party still accuses the other of being a liar about last year's trip, as if it was just yesterday.

This year dad says, "I'm off work. You went last year and didn't even tell me about it so I am going this year. Besides, it falls on *my day*, Wednesday." Mom will be quick to point out that *technically*, Wednesday, is her *day* with Billy *until* school lets out and dad picks him up at 5:00 p.m. She will politely advise Dad that he can feel free to pick Billy up early on Wednesday since he has made arrangements to be off from work. When she gets back from the pumpkin patch and hayride with Billy, Dad can take him at 3:00 p.m. instead of 5:00 p.m., so they can have a little "extra time" together. Dad won't hear of it.

Some possible outcomes for field trips when there is moderate to high conflict between the parents:

- Both go and it is a disaster (easy to imagine).
- Both go and there is no scene. However, everyone is so tense that it isn't fun for the child or anyone else who knows that there is parental discord.
- Both go and the poor child is torn between which one he should be spending time with throughout the day and the trip is a disappointment for him.
- Both go and one parent hogs the child all day, leaving emotional damage for the left-out parent to deal with in addition to the child's level of disappointment and confusion.
- Other parents, teachers, and children now know more than they need to know about your situation.

It is possible to make field trips enjoyable and memorable for your children — and for you too. To do so, it's probably best to take turns going. Hopefully, the two of you have the communication skills and respect for your child to make that happen. If one parent cannot take their turn or chooses not to, the other parent should go if available. If that happens and one parent has now possibly had two turns in a row, the next trip should go to the one who has not yet gone — regardless of whose "turn" it is to go. Share.

By taking turns, it is possible to shield your child from the reality that the two of you collectively may ruin the field trip experience if you both go. If your child is young, you could simply explain that both of you would like to go, but one of you has to go to work. Taking turns with field trips is a great way to show that you are secure with your parent-child relationship by letting your child know that you want her and mommy or daddy to have a good time together and that you and your child will likely go on the next one together or maybe you will soon do something special too.

If both parents decide to go, there are some ways to avoid disaster. First, do not ride the bus together. If one goes on the bus, the other one should drive there separately. If you both attend, take shifts and divide the time or events as equitably as possible, dis-

TIME FOR ADVICE

The best time to give advice to your children is while they're still young enough to believe you know what you are talking about.

cussing as much as you can before the trip and not in the presence of your child. Make yourself scarce at times to allow your child and the other parent some time to spend uninterrupted and unobserved. Go make that important phone call or go back to the car for some reason. Better yet, let everyone know that you have to miss the first half of the trip and that you will get there at lunch time or some other breaking point. The other parent should then "back off" for a while and give you space with your child. If you are together at any time in the presence of your child, you would be wise to only discuss the event or the sights on the trip.

For example, if the three of you are at the zoo, it is fine to say something like, "Look at the monkey," or ask open-ended questions like, "What do you think the monkey is doing?" Keep the conversation light and focused on the trip. Obviously, it would not be appropriate to say, "Hey, doesn't that monkey look just like daddy?" Similarly, if Billy asks if he can have an ice cream cone, it would be inappropriate for dad to say, "Ask your mom, she sucks all my money from me, so I can't afford to eat." Things will likely just go downhill from there. If you can't resist making snide comments, you shouldn't be on a field trip together.

If you can successfully avoid the pitfalls, field trips provide great opportunities to:

> REALITY
> CHECK
>
> Show your children
> that you care about
> how they feel.
> Realize that through your
> words *and* actions
> they come to know you
> and your philosophy of life.

- ☞ Be mindful of and learn to focus on how your parental interaction affects the good times of your children and those in the vicinity.
- ☞ Learn to operate by frameworks or understandings as opposed to binding agreements regarding who should go on any given field trip.
- ☞ Practice parental flexibility in adjusting schedules and events for your child's benefit.
- ☞ Enjoy special moments and events with your child and make meaningful and happy memories.
- ☞ Take plenty of happy pictures and videos of you and your child.

Sports & Other Activities

33

Sports involvement and other extracurricular activities (such as Boy Scouts and Girl Scouts, dance, piano lessons, and so forth) can be another source of trouble between separated and divorced parents. Sometimes it even seems that parents go out of their way to ruin these experiences for their children. Those problems often stem from a parent's skewed understanding of "their" time with the children.

The good and bad part of court-ordered schedules for separated parents can simply be the fact that there is a court-ordered schedule. The advantage of one is that it can minimize the jerking around that often occurs regarding the division of parental time. However, there are times when it works as a double-edged sword for the children. Let's look at an example.

Don was one of the most annoying clients that I have ever represented, but I've learned that his antics are quite commonplace. His court-ordered visitation was what is sadly often referred to as typical daddy visitation — every other weekend, Wednesday night dinner, some shared holidays, and a one- or two-week vacation in the summer. Whoopee! For someone who really wants to be involved with their children and has the availability and re-

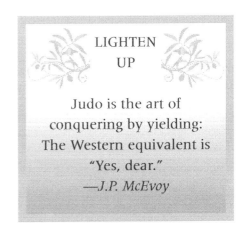

LIGHTEN
UP

Judo is the art of conquering by yielding: The Western equivalent is "Yes, dear."
—*J.P. McEvoy*

sources to do so, this type of schedule is lame. Don, like many fathers who have such limited involvement forced upon them, was bitter.

Don's ex-wife hated him and never had a good thing to say about him. If Sally had her way, little Katie would probably never have anything to do with her father. If Don wanted time with his daughter, he needed to be on his best behavior, but he didn't do himself any favors when it came to his daughter's sports and extracurricular activities. In retaliation for what he perceived to be an injustice about everything, Don would go out of his way to make life difficult for Sally. Unfortunately, if this meant using Katie, it didn't matter.

Sally was a very involved mother and kept her daughter involved in all sorts of activities — from Brownies to soccer to ballet. But Don saw any activity that happened to fall on "his" scheduled time with Katie as a personal affront. Knowing how strongly Sally felt about having Katie enjoy friends and activities, Don could rarely resist the temptation to make other plans, no matter how trivial, to keep Katie from her scheduled activities when she was with him.

In Don's mind, Sally had no right to expect that he should permit Katie to participate in anything. After all, it was *his* time and he didn't have enough of it. Therefore, he reasoned that on *his* time, *he* gets to make such decisions. By disrupting Katie's favorite pastimes, his daughter ultimately came to believe what her mother constantly drilled into her head: "Dad is a jerk."

A similar sad story involves a little boy who loved and excelled at baseball. Ricky was one of those children you just knew could be destined for the baseball hall of fame with the proper guidance. Since Ricky got his start in tee-ball, his dad had attended every practice. Even-

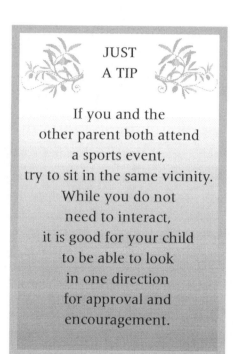

JUST A TIP

If you and the other parent both attend a sports event, try to sit in the same vicinity. While you do not need to interact, it is good for your child to be able to look in one direction for approval and encouragement.

tually he worked as an assistant coach for Ricky's teams.

Ricky's parents went through years of litigation, beginning when Ricky was a toddler. Although the judge awarded shared physical custody, he awarded the dad, Richard, sole legal custody. This entitled the dad to final decision-making authority. However, as a precondition to this arrangement, Richard was court-ordered to consult with and consider the opinions of Ricky's mother before making any major decisions.

The court order also required each parent to transport Ricky to his regular activities. If an activity fell on "dad's time" it was his responsibility to get his son to and from that activity; mom had the same court-ordered requirement. Ricky's father had requested this provision due to the difficulties that the mother made out of taking Ricky to scheduled activities that fell on *her* time. These two terms of the court order always irritated Ricky's mom, Deanna. She was not terribly interested in attending such events and did not really encourage her son's involvement.

A few years after the custody decision, Ricky was eligible to play on the advanced travel baseball team. This would allow Ricky to play more often in a competitive environment with high caliber coaches. Ricky and all of his baseball buddies were excited about the upcoming season. Deanna, however, did not agree and she made it clear that *she* was not going to participate in travel baseball. Her stated reasons were nonsense — it was too dangerous, it was too much traveling, and it would impinge on her "family time" with Ricky. The real reasons had more to do with jealousy, bitterness, and an attempt to exert control.

REALITY CHECK

While things occasionally come up (such as a family reunion, a funeral, or a special person's birthday celebration) that will require missing scheduled sports games, practices, or activities, you should make it a point to actively participate and encourage involvement in activities that benefit your children. When your children are scheduled to be with you, it is your responsibility to make it happen. Be responsible; be a winner in your child's eyes.

Richard had to remind Deanna that the court order required each party to take Ricky to his regular activities, including Ricky's sports involvement. In addition, he reminded her that he had the final decision-making authority on important matters pertaining to Ricky's health, education, religious upbringing, and general welfare. Things got ugly. Deanna's response was that travel baseball was not a regular sports activity and therefore she was not required to take Ricky on her scheduled time. Furthermore, she did not regard this as a significantly important matter that Richard had the right to settle against her wishes. She further stated that certainly Ricky could attend on his father's time but not on *her* time. Deanna would not budge and advised her ex to take her to court if he didn't like it.

After filing for contempt proceedings and realizing that another round of litigation would likely snowball out of control, this dad made a difficult decision. He did not enroll his son in the travel league. Richard knew that by the time the case came up for a hearing the baseball season would have come and gone. In the interim, Ricky would be disappointed at intermittent participation. Furthermore, sporadic attendance wasn't acceptable at that level of play. There was nothing to gain by forcing the issue, so the father dropped the proceedings. Deanna had won! Her son had lost out.

During this difficult period, parents may be preoccupied with their own problems, but they continue to be the most important people in their children's lives. Your ongoing commitment to your children's well-being is vital.

Why would any decent parent sabotage their children's participation in sports and special activities? When it comes to your children's activities, do remember the following:

- These activities are for the children — they're not for you, although you can enjoy them.
- Sports and other personally satisfying activities are healthy and rewarding experiences for children.
- Regular exercise decreases the risk of heart disease and osteoporosis and reduces the risk of emotional problems such as depression and anxiety.

☞ Evidence suggests that physically healthy children are more likely to mature into physically active adults, and that is a good thing.

☞ When a parent attends sports and extracurricular activities, children feel important and valued.

☞ Taking your children to sports activities is a parental responsibility — just do it!

☞ There is really no such thing as *your* time; it is the children's time with the parent that counts.

☞ Watching your children participate in activities that they enjoy is a very satisfying use of your time.

☞ By encouraging, watching, and supporting your children's participation, it gives you and your children something to talk about. This can be a great conversation starting point for all kinds of issues — good sportsmanship, sharing, responsibility, and work ethic.

☞ Be proactive. You can help your child enjoy participating in sports.

☞ What will your child ultimately think about you for interfering in his or her enjoyment of such activities?

For more information on children and sports (and a host of other family issues) visit: www.familymanagement.com.

If you and your ex can be civil enough to handle it, both of you can attend the games or other activities. Be sure not to use game time as an opportunity to discuss anything about anything with the other parent. Just enjoy the experience of watching and supporting your child. Do show good sportsmanship and proper manners by at least being cordial to one another.

Practice and game schedules can be demanding. The commitment can be difficult to follow through with — especially when *you* didn't even make the commitment! You may feel frustrated.

You may feel torn about making a sacrifice of your time. You may feel like striking back at your ex. But think of the commitment as your child's. Your child has made a commitment to a team or an activity. Help him or her to follow through.

34

Medical Appointments & Records

Access to medical records, choosing healthcare providers, and parental inclusion or exclusion in children's medical treatment can be a hot-button issue. Pediatricians especially despise being placed in the middle of parental discord, and many doctors will refuse to treat children of parents who appear to be using the doctor's office as an evidentiary case-building exercise. The problems generally arise and intensify when one parent acts in a unilateral or self-promoting manner. If both parents have access to information and consultation with healthcare providers *and* share information when appropriate, there is less room for exploitation, contention, and litigation involving your children's medical issues.

In my nearly twenty years as an attorney, I've identified eight basic types of disputes related to medical issues in custody cases:

1. A power play over decision-making authority
2. The desire to conceal something of possible significance that is contained in a medical record
3. The desire to use something in a medical record in a "sandbagging" or surreptitious manner

LIGHTEN UP

A little boy went up to his mother and asked, "Mom, where did all of my intelligence come from?" The mother replied, "Well son, you must have gotten it from your father, because I still have mine."

4. Attempts to make one parent look better than the other by "demonstrating" that he or she is the primary caretaker
5. Attempts to allege parental inattentiveness
6. Arguments about what is medically important
7. Health insurance issues
8. Other medical financial issues or extraordinary expenses

Some of these areas of disagreement are simply a result of the communication difficulties between parents, but others are used more disingenuously as part of a case-building campaign. Regardless of the motive or intent of parents in medical disputes involving their children, such tactics have no place in positive parenting and they should be avoided.

I have seen parents refuse to pay for or contribute to children's medical bills because they were not informed of the visit or did not approve of it. Another common dig is illustrated when one parent has a habit of telling the other that a medical appointment is "none of your business" or that he or she is inept at tending to such responsibilities. In more contentious cases, a parent will simply take a child for an "examination" to document innocent bruising, diaper rash, or "suspicious markings." One could call it medical provider abuse; it's an appointment that a parent would never consider if it were not for the fact that there may be a custody case to bolster.

Often parents want to create a good rapport with pediatricians simply to have the file documented. For example, a pediatric file may be

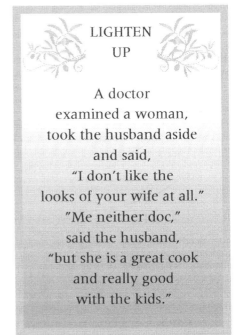

LIGHTEN
UP

A doctor
examined a woman,
took the husband aside
and said,
"I don't like the
looks of your wife at all."
"Me neither doc,"
said the husband,
"but she is a great cook
and really good
with the kids."

used to show that mommy, not daddy, has brought little Johnny in for all of his regularly scheduled well visits, all of his shots and immunizations, and all periodic physical examinations. Therefore, it must be reasoned, she is a wonderful and concerned parent. Since the good doctor has never met "daddy," she can only attest to mother's parenting. In the scheme of things, judges really do not care who makes the appointment and who attends. They do, however, care a great deal when it appears that one parent is deliberately keeping the other parent in the dark or using the child's medical treatment to build a stronger custody case.

There are a few simple guidelines to ensure that the pediatrician's office is not abused and that you're not simply using a child's medical appointments and issues to serve your own needs. There is no excuse for bad behavior when it comes to medical issues. But

I know parents who've done things that should never be done, so a few reminders are in order.

Medical Dos

- ☞ Make sure to inform the other parent about all medical appointments and any related issues. When possible, these things should be discussed in advance and decisions should be made jointly.
- ☞ Keep the other parent fully informed if you are the one who is making the decisions — whether by virtue of past practice, agreement, or court order.
- ☞ Understand that your children's medical providers will not want to be called as witnesses in any court hearing.
- ☞ Be aware of and get involved in your children's medical needs.
- ☞ Allow the other parent to get involved in your children's medical needs.
- ☞ Provide the doctor's office with a written document allowing the doctor and staff to communicate with either parent.
- ☞ Make certain that the doctor's office has complete contact information for both parents.
- ☞ Be sure that there is a clear understanding of whose health insurance is to be billed and who will pay for co-pays and uncovered items.
- ☞ Whoever takes the child to the appointment should be prepared to pay the co-pay or non-insured items.
- ☞ Occasionally offer the other parent the opportunity to take the children to their appointments, without you having to be present. You can also alternate attendance at some appointments so that the children feel that each parent is concerned and attentive to their medical needs.

- Keep things in perspective. Not everything is a medical emergency.
- Honor any standing agreements about reimbursing the other parent for up-front expenditures.
- If verbal communication is not optimal, obtain a copy of the office note before you leave and fax or mail it to the other parent and be sure to include any other relevant comments or instructions the doctor may have provided to you while you were there.

Medical Don'ts

- Never bad-mouth or belittle the other parent to the doctor or the doctor's staff.
- Do not talk about the other parent, your separation, divorce, or other non-medical issues with the doctor. (He or she isn't interested anyway.)
- Don't tell the doctor to send the bill to the other parent.
- Don't tell the doctor not to talk to the other parent.
- Don't hide or withhold medical information from the other parent.
- Don't make appointments without at least informing the other parent (in advance if possible).
- Don't schedule appointments that fall on the other parent's time without prior discussion.
- Don't schedule medical appointments on dates and times when you know the other parent cannot attend.
- Don't assume that the other parent is not interested in medical issues.
- Don't use the doctor's office for any purpose other than to provide quality health care for your children.

☞ Don't discuss anything other than the medical visit if both of you are attending the medical appointment. This is no time for general discussions or arguments.

The Right Thing

When approaching medical issues you should keep in mind that when there is a separation, things change. The norms and practices of the past may no longer apply. For example, if you were always the parent that did everything in the realm of medical appointments, do not assume that the other parent

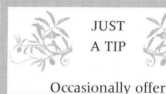

JUST A TIP

Occasionally offer the other parent the opportunity to take the children to their appointments, without you having to be present. Or consider alternating attendance at some appointments so that the children feel that each parent is concerned and attentive to their medical needs.

is unable or unwilling to participate. Do not assume that he or she now is trying to be actively involved just to look good in case there is a court hearing. Even if that is the reason, don't worry about it; you will be doing the right thing by encouraging the other parent's participation.

35

Sickness & Medical Issues

L ike Mother's Day and Father's Day, when it comes to a child's illness or medical emergency, it is once again truce time. It saddens me when I remember the experience my ex-wife and I had at the hospital emergency room when my son needed stitches in his chin for the second time after falling off of his bicycle.

To my ex-wife's credit, she did notify me *before* making it to the hospital. I dropped everything and made it to the emergency room before our son was examined by the doctor. Unfortunately, once there we both behaved badly.

It is indeed a sad commentary when the interactions of a child's parents overshadow the significance of the necessity for medical attention.

When your child is sick:

- Consider if it is in the child's best interests to travel to and from each parent.
- If you and the other parent disagree on whether visitation should be cancelled and if you are still in the counting-days-and-hours mode, consider agreeing on make-up time as soon as the child is feeling better.
- Make sure that medicine travels with the child, with all proper instructions and a note indicating when the last dosage was administered.
- Notify the other parent in advance about any medical issues so he or she can be prepared and adjust plans accordingly.

In the event of a medical emergency:

- Notify the other parent as soon as possible, preferably while on the way to emergency care.
- Never lie or misrepresent the facts concerning an accident or injury.
- Always provide love and attention to your child and avoid insinuating parental ineffectiveness or casting blame if the child was injured on the other parent's watch. Children do get injured even under the best supervision.

36

Dating & New Relationships

When separated parents do not get along, throwing a new relationship into the mix can become messy. There is a time and a place for beginning new relationships. Generally, right after the breakup is not the time to introduce your children to new partners, especially if it is likely to inflame the current parenting situation. Special care generally needs to be taken in dealing with an ex if a new person is going to be around your children or otherwise become involved in your parent-to-parent communication issues. Almost without exception, the amount of time and the type of interaction that any "newcomer" has with your children is sure to provoke some "emotional responses" from the other parent.

There are good reasons to be cautious. First, exposing youngsters and adolescents to new romantic relationships can be very confusing to children of recently separated parents. Secondly, no matter who left who in the breakup, it generally causes some emotional reaction when a former partner is seeing someone else and that new person is around your children. It throws a whole new dynamic into an already emotionally charged situation. Thirdly, having a new boyfriend or girlfriend around

WISE WORDS

I am too shy
to express my sexual needs
except over the phone
to people I don't know.
—*Gary Shandling*

is an imposition on your children's time with you and they often resent it no matter what they tell you.

When you separate, your children need your love, understanding, and attention more than ever. You and the other parent have changed your children's lives forever. Children do not expect to have their parents break up. They do not understand it and they often feel as if the breakup has much more to do with them than it does. Let's face it, a separation is often about one person's wants and needs not getting met by the other. It is about selfishness and self-fulfillment. In past generations, it was common for married couples to sacrifice their happiness for as much as twenty years or longer until the children were grown. In many ways such love for one's children is admirable.

Most parents say they would do anything for their children. So why is it often so difficult for newly separated parents to avoid mixing dating and children? While I guess those issues might be better left to the therapists, there are some important things to be mindful of when it comes to balancing your needs and those of your children.

- Your children will be confused if you add a new relationship shortly after separation.
- Your children need you most at this crucial time.
- Your divided time will detract from quality time, because no one can serve two masters.

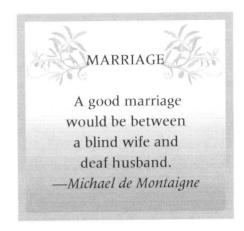

MARRIAGE

A good marriage
would be between
a blind wife and
deaf husband.
—*Michael de Montaigne*

- The other parent may likely disapprove and this will also affect the children.
- The courts frown upon it in many circumstances.
- You may be on the rebound anyway and not exercising your best judgment.
- There is a time for work and a time for play. Single parenting is work, and to be successful in anything the work comes first.
- Your life has changed and it needs to be reshaped — and that takes time.

While it is nice to move on in your interpersonal relationships, you should be very cautious in encouraging anyone new to bond with your children. There is no substitute for *your* time and attention. Do your thing when your children are with the other parent. When your children are with you, spend that time wisely — with them.

37

Stepparents & Significant Others

When you do find a person that you click with (not in the Internet dating sense of "click with") and it appears likely that this person will be elevated to at least the "significant other" status, special care needs to be taken for the benefit of the children regarding such a relationship. For our purposes the term *significant other* means more than casual dating. It refers to a long-term, committed relationship (perhaps live in) that may lead to marriage or a life partnership.

Here are a few tips for mixing these relationships with the children.

- ☞ The roles of all of the individuals need to be clearly defined, or at least understood, and boundaries need to be observed and respected.
- ☞ The parents must learn to deal with each other directly.

- ☞ The new person really has no "standing" to be the messenger, negotiator, or spokesperson for either side.

- ☞ If any issues or concerns can be resolved or addressed by and between both parents, this new person should not get involved in much of anything with the other parent.

- ☞ At transition time, keep new romantic interests out of the picture. The other parent probably doesn't even want to have to look at you, and he or she is almost certainly even less happy to see your new friend.

- ☞ Some feelings of jealousy from your ex are fairly natural when it comes to the children forming a relationship with your new significant other. Recognize this and do not exacerbate the situation. You may feel the same way one day.

- ☞ Messages going to and through the "newcomer" should be avoided.

- ☞ Never encourage your child to refer to anyone else as mom or dad.

The new person, irrespective of the relationship formed with the children, needs to exercise great restraint in identifying and accepting his or her proper place in the dynamics of the situation to avoid a host of problems that may result from the mixed and changing relationships. If the two parents have significant "communication issues," any emotionally involved third wheel is more often than not going to be an unproductive addition to the communication equation.

Unfortunately, when parents have a tendency to put their children in the middle of adult conflicts, they are also likely to put newcomers in the middle. In addition to straining this new adult relationship, it will generally keep the children in the middle. The new person would be wise to take a back seat.

In general it's best to minimize the role of the newcomer in the area of parent-to-parent communications, but sometimes the new person interacts with the other parent better than the two biological parents interact with each other. This is fine — *if it works*. Remember, what is best for the children is whatever works best for the children.

Children want to be loved. When they can trust and enjoy the benefits of a stable significant other in one or both of their parents' lives, it can work out well for them. It really can. The key is not to introduce that person too soon. It's also vitally important that the significant other recognize boundaries and allow the relationship with the children to develop at its own pace. Every child is different; be patient.

What if your ex has a new relationship? Well, look for the positives. Hopefully that person can set a good example and be one more person to love and positively contribute to your children's lives. If not, then try not to dwell on it. Some things are out of your hands. Focus on what you *can* do — love your children and make the most of the time you have together.

On a personal note, I am very grateful for the relationship that developed between my son and his Deb, the woman who became my second (*and final*) wife. She takes a lot of delight in Nicholas, and they have always had their own special relationship that they both greatly value and appreciate. I cannot imagine a more perfect stepmom.

38

Making Memories

Remember the Cleaver family? Ward, June, Wally, and the Beaver? June was the devoted stay-at-home mom. Consequently, the overwhelming amount of parenting and "hands-on" time with the children came from her. Ward worked all day, came home in the evening, ate his dinner, read the paper, and maybe tucked the boys in for bed. There was the around-the-dinner-table, "how was your day" small talk and such, but even Ward Cleaver didn't spend too much time with his boys. He was, however, the one who had the unpleasant duty of dealing with the more serious discipline issues. Remember the old saying, "Ward, I think you were a little hard on the Beaver last night?"

Nonetheless, I bet if June had left Ward, the amount of time that he would have made for his children when they were with him would have at least doubled. The fact is that in a "traditional" two-parent household, the father may spend far less time with his children than if he only had "visitation" rights every other weekend and one or two evenings during the week. There is something about knowing that you have a limited amount of time with your children that makes you spend it wisely. It is similar to the way we can get so much work done just before leaving for vacation.

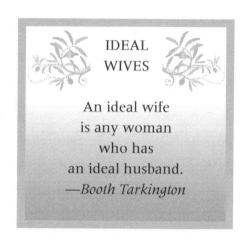

IDEAL WIVES

An ideal wife
is any woman
who has
an ideal husband.
—*Booth Tarkington*

By virtue of the separation you will have less available time to choose from to spend with your children. However, you can and may be more likely to spend more actual time with your children. When you are with them, you should devote all of your time and energy to building upon and strengthening the parent-child relationship. When your children are with the other parent, hope that he or she does the same.

As children my sister and I never really wanted for anything. We were, perhaps, somewhat spoiled, but certainly not spoiled brats. We were well cared for, and we always felt an abundance of love in and out of our middle-class home. Our parents taught by example and disciplined us with love and reason. We were blessed to have such wonderful parents and a fun-filled childhood. I think my sister was in the sixth grade before she realized that Santa Claus did not land on our roof with a bunch of reindeer and squeeze his fat ass down our chimney with a sack of toys.

In high school some of my classmates could not believe the things that my parents and I discussed. We were, and still are, great friends. I remember, though, a time when I was feeling pretty cocky and thought my parents were being unfair about something. Dad very clearly explained that our house was a dictatorship, not a democracy. Years later, during a few difficult times in my life, my father professed that my happiness had always been his main concern. Now I understand it from the other side.

> **WISE WORDS**
>
> The little reed, bending to the forces of the wind, soon stood upright again when the storm had passed over.
> —*Aesop*

Parenting is one of the most important jobs that you will ever have. There is no reason why it cannot also be one of the most rewarding, exciting, and fulfilling experiences that life has to offer. It is also important to remember that not every interaction between parent and children must be turned into a "learning experience." Some of the most precious moments between parents and children are those that are unplanned.

There is no higher calling, no worthier task, no greater commitment required than to raise happy and healthy children. The degree to which we are successful in shaping the human lives that are entrusted to us will shape the course of world history. Life is short; we need to enjoy every step along the way. Even during some of my most difficult times of parenting through separation and divorce, I created and held onto priceless parenting memories. There is no greater feeling than enjoying the loving moments between a parent and a child. Even making peeing swords in the toilet together can be an awesome experience for a toddler and his dad. (It's a guy thing.)

You may not be the Cleavers, but your new family dynamics can create plenty of opportunities to enjoy special moments. While you may occasionally feel sadness and grief that your children spend some of their time living apart from you, don't dwell on it. Remember, it could be worse, much worse.

When your children are with you, make it count. Each day they're with you is an opportunity for great experiences. Make plans and look forward to the next time you're together. The options are limitless. Memories don't have to cost money. Younger children love arts and crafts.

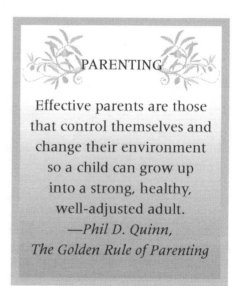

PARENTING

Effective parents are those that control themselves and change their environment so a child can grow up into a strong, healthy, well-adjusted adult.
—*Phil D. Quinn,*
The Golden Rule of Parenting

Go on picnics together; enjoy bike rides on summer days and hot chocolate and movies on cold winter nights. There are many activities that can be lots of fun to experience with your children. You may even get creative and take your children to help out at a soup kitchen during the holiday season for example. Perhaps cut down a Christmas tree together each year or plan annual nature weekend camping trips or start other parent-child rituals or family traditions. It's okay to play just for the fun of it. However, when it comes to "adults only" activities, remember, if you are going to be hard on the beaver, make sure the children aren't around!

39

A Kinder & Gentler Approach:
Collaborative Law

In recent years, a new breed of family law attorneys has evolved; perhaps for you, it's happened just in time! About half of all marriages in the United States end in divorce. The sad reality is that divorce involves far too many complex personal and family issues to be adequately addressed and appropriately resolved by an already overwhelmed judiciary. People need to learn to help themselves. Fortunately, the collaborative law method provides the tools, resources, and professional assistance in a specialized and structured framework to achieve effective outcomes for families in transition.

Furthermore, it is no secret that even under the best of circumstances, divorce and child custody and visitation issues often result in emotional upheavals. Divorce professionals and researchers alike have concluded that *how* a couple conducts themselves during a divorce has far greater impact on their children than the separation itself.

Many collaborative professionals view the collaborative
law model as a commitment
to a principled, negotiated settlement, focusing on client
empowerment, with estab-
lished protocols and without
the threat or use of court action. Collaborative divorce, as
it is sometimes referred to, includes a commitment to recognize that divorce is multi-
dimensional, and it presents

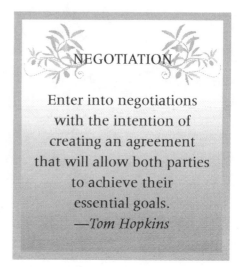

NEGOTIATION

Enter into negotiations
with the intention of
creating an agreement
that will allow both parties
to achieve their
essential goals.
—*Tom Hopkins*

opportunities to provide resources for couples and families to assist with the parental, communication, and financial issues that are
just part of the process.

The Collaborative Way to Divorce by Stuart G. Webb, the founder
of the collaborative law movement, and Ronald D. Ousky, an early
pioneer of the process, describes the origin and development of the
collaborative law movement and guides you through the steps of
the collaborative process so that you can make better, more informed, and more strategic decisions — resulting in a win-win outcome for you and your family. Stressing cooperation over confrontation and resolution over revenge, collaborative divorce is
quickly transforming how couples dissolve their marriages, divide
their assets, and reinvent their post-divorce parenting relationships.

Collaborative law practices take place outside of the court
process. It is a transparent, good faith, open, and honest process.
In addition, the parties, who must choose to go through the process,
commit to avoid litigation and utilize specially trained attorneys
and/or a team approach to resolving conflict in an atmosphere of
honesty, cooperation, integrity, and professionalism. All disclosure

is voluntary, full, and honest, and all experts or non-legal professionals work as consultants for the entire group.

Given the voluntary nature of participation in this process, coupled with specialized training of the attorneys, the parties themselves are able

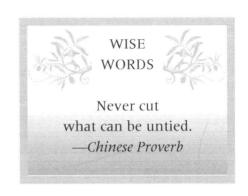

WISE WORDS

Never cut
what can be untied.
—*Chinese Proverb*

to completely control the process, the outcome, and their futures. Nothing is left to chance and all decisions are reached voluntarily. Family matters can remain private matters. Selection of experts, such as appraisers, financial planners, and mental health professionals, can be made individually or as part of the collaborative divorce process. Given this framework, and governed by the voluntary nature of the process, suspicion and paranoia about the other side's strategy or intentions decline dramatically.

Initially, a collaborative lawyer will lay a foundation for successful representation by communicating a great deal of information to the client about the process. There are clear expectations that need to be adopted by all parties so that resolution of all disputes can be conducted in a civilized manner. Many of the negotiations are done in a four-way setting with each participant being represented by counsel throughout the process. The parties, therefore, do not "hide" behind their lawyers. There is a loosely structured choreography that is followed by the collaborative law professionals, and there are pre- and post-meeting sessions between a single attorney and his or her client. The two attorneys themselves may sometimes meet to discuss ways to resolve issues in an amicable and collaborative fashion. Unlike a traditional litigation setting, the opposing attorney can speak directly to the other lawyer's client in four-way meetings. This maximizes the group's potential for creative problem solving and exposes any obstacles to resolution.

It is estimated that most collaborative law cases take between two and ten four-way meetings before resolution. The final stages of the process involve the attorneys

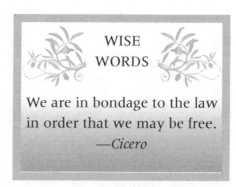

WISE WORDS

We are in bondage to the law in order that we may be free.
—Cicero

handling technical tasks of preparing court papers and written agreements. The process usually concludes with a four-way meeting to help clients reflect upon their successes, generosity, and acts of goodwill, and to discuss their combined protocol for handling future issues and disputes. If nothing else, this last meeting symbolizes a ceremonial marker, a finalization of a unique process with a successful outcome.

The collaborative process includes the following benefits:

- Keeps your children out of adult conflicts and minimizes the overall controversy
- Provides you with greater control over the outcome of your divorce
- Is generally less expensive and quicker than litigation
- Helps maintain a sense of integrity and respect between the parties
- Is a private and confidential process
- Increases interpersonal communication skills
- Promotes open and honest communication
- Significantly reduces stress and uncertainty
- Provides a positive parenting framework for the future
- Increases the likelihood of raising happier and emotionally healthier children

☞ Provides effective solutions to one of life's most difficult challenges

WISE WORDS

Regret is an appalling
waste of energy;
you can't build on it;
it's only good for
wallowing in.
—*Katherine Mansfield*

In *Collaborative Divorce, The Revolutionary New Way to Restructure Your Family, Resolve Legal Issues, and Move on with Your Life*, Pauline Tesler and Peggy Thompson, two collaborative law innovators who train professionals around the world, walk you through the stages of collaborative divorce while stressing the team approach. Time and time again, they have found that with the assistance of two lawyers trained in collaborative law, two coaches, a financial consultant, and a child specialist (when needed), a separating couple will be able to focus on the needs of everyone who will be directly affected by the divorce. This paradigm shift away from adversarial litigation empowers you — not lawyers or a judge— to shape the outcome of your divorce.

Collaborative law provides an opportunity for continued mutual respect between the divorcing parties, both through and after divorce. By working together, collaborative divorce allows both parties to move on with their lives with dignity and peace as they struggle to raise their children in two separate households.

Through the collaborative process, parents learn and practice open communication, self-management, and negotiation skills, which can form the basis for successful future interactions. Through collaboration, parents learn to manage and reduce conflict and the anguish and divided loyalties it engenders in children. Through collaboration, parents have the opportunity to lay the foundation for the respectful, cooperative parenting of their children.

One of the most difficult aspects of divorce is the redefining of parental roles. To help children transition successfully during and after divorce, parents must learn to set aside their anger and disappointment with each other and learn to parent together. Parents must

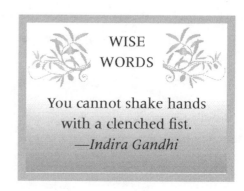

WISE WORDS

You cannot shake hands with a clenched fist.
—*Indira Gandhi*

come to agreement on sharing time with and responsibility for their children. They must respect the children's right to be with the other parent and the other set of grandparents and relatives. They must find ways for both families to attend school events, sporting activities, and teachers meetings, as well as share birthdays and holidays.

The goal is to create a new family system that supports the children and provides them with necessary stability. When parents continue to act together in their children's best interests, they make it possible for their children to make a healthy adjustment to the divorce and any changes that come later. Parents may separate and wish to sever ties, but children are irrevocably tied to *both* parents and those ties must be maintained if the child is to emerge from divorce happy and healthy. Those of us who practice collaborative family law believe collaborative divorce can become the new norm in America. For additional resources and information on collaborative law, see appendix E as well as the website of the International Academy of Collaborative Professionals (www.collaborativepractice.com).

Choosing the Right Attorney

While collaborative law is not for everyone or every situation, special care should always be taken when hiring an attorney to represent you in a family law case. Once you have met with the attorney, explained your case, and had your questions answered, there are some questions you should ask yourself:

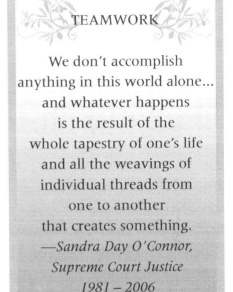

TEAMWORK

We don't accomplish
anything in this world alone...
and whatever happens
is the result of the
whole tapestry of one's life
and all the weavings of
individual threads from
one to another
that creates something.
—*Sandra Day O'Connor,*
Supreme Court Justice
1981 – 2006

- Will I feel comfortable working closely with this person?
- Do I feel confident in the lawyer's experience and level of skill to handle my case?
- Do I understand the lawyer's explanation of what my case involves?
- Do I understand the proposed fee agreement?
- Do I trust this person to handle my most personal matters?

If you feel comfortable with the attorney and confident that their experience is adequate for your case, you have probably found a good match. Asking and answering the above questions will go a long way in determining if this is the right attorney for you.

Hopefully, with the basic introduction to collaborative law you can begin to see that it sure beats the alternatives of going to court in a contested case. If you cannot grasp this, perhaps you are the stumbling block to an amicable resolution. For the sake of your children, I hope not.

Getting on Board

One of the most frustrating feelings that superior parents face during a tumultuous separation and divorce occurs when they "get it" — and the other side doesn't. When you realize that there is nothing to gain by constantly and continually fighting over and about your children and their parent-child relationships, you will want to do all that you can to collaborate, cooperate, and compromise when appropriate. Once you realize that the goal is to make life better for you and your children, it can become truly frustrating to deal with an ex who doesn't realize that. When the other parent is still in fight mode, peaceful resolutions are few and far between. Progress is often short lived.

So, how *do* you get the other parent on board with superior parenting? Quite simply, if the other parent is drowning in their own misery (and trying to drown everyone else too), you need to throw the other parent a metaphoric lifeline. (No, not the one with the heavy weight attached to it.) Basically, unless you help the other parent get on board, all of your best intentions will be of minimal consequence.

Here is one of the best ways to promote and foster positive parental action. Search out articles and books on topics about separation and divorce and its effects on children. Learn how to be a better communicator, a better listener. Learn how to put

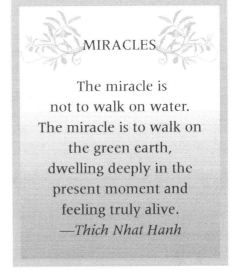

MIRACLES

The miracle is
not to walk on water.
The miracle is to walk on
the green earth,
dwelling deeply in the
present moment and
feeling truly alive.
—*Thich Nhat Hanh*

things into perspective. Work on you. Decide to be the best parent that you can be under whatever circumstances you find yourself. Learn to accept what you cannot change and to change what you can. Attend co-parenting workshops, lectures, and seminars. Listen to the CDs and watch DVDs. In short, become a student of positive parenting.

Gather as many resources as you can. Sift through it all and when you find gems, share them. That's right — share them with the other parent. You see, usually the parent most in need of help and guidance doesn't recognize it. After all, everything is your fault, right? Sound familiar? Well, no one like that wants to be outdone, especially by a no-good scoundrel like you. Are you following me here?

So, if you let the other parent know that you have done this, read that, signed up for a class, or purchased something they have not, sooner or later their desire to be in control may just lead them down the right path. They may get there only because they think that you are "up to something," but it doesn't matter how or why they get there. They just need to hear enough of the right information from the right people. If that takes some direct help or even surreptitious assistance from you, so be it. It is for the betterment of your children's lives and it sure would make yours run smoother if the other parent practiced some of what you already know. It is truly in helping others that we help ourselves.

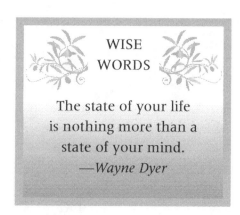

WISE WORDS

The state of your life is nothing more than a state of your mind.
—*Wayne Dyer*

Remember though, generally, if you suggest ideas and options, you may not get heard. It won't register with some. It is very helpful when someone else — an authority, an expert, or anyone for that matter — provides your ex with valuable information. Use the power of third party edification. Then, hope and pray that some of it sinks in. Act in conformity with what you have learned and leave the powers of persuasion to someone else.

In some situations, you may choose to write the other parent a short, non-judgmental note that refers them to something that, if followed, would be helpful.

Here is an example:

Dear Wilma:

I recently read a good book and it has caused me to stop and reflect on the past as well as think about the present and future. I feel there are many things that could be improved upon when it comes to the way we interact as parents to our children, especially during these challenging times. Wilma, you may have the enclosed copy of *Stop Fighting Over the Kids: Resolving Day-*

to-Day Custody Conflict in Divorce Situations. Reading this taught me a lot. In many instances, I saw myself and I have recognized some areas that I would like to improve upon. I will continue to look for resources like this to improve our future co-parenting. I imagine you, too, have done some research on related topics. I invite you to share any information that you think would be helpful. I just thought that it might be good if we both hear and evaluate the same information. Thanks for listening.

Sincerely,
Fred

To the High Road

Where are we and where do we need to go? Hopefully, by now you feel as though you have been provided with valuable information and useful resources. How you choose to use this information is up to you.

No one can live your life. Both you and your children will live with the consequences of your choices and your actions when it comes to parenting through these tumultuous times.

Separation and divorce are life-changing events, especially when there are children involved. Expect that you will feel "lost" for some time. This is normal. Life is going to be different than you had envisioned, but that can be good. Remember, the path that you were on prior to separation from your children's other parent was not leading you to a happy and healthy place. Find *your* Big Rock. There are many paths to get you there. I commend you for taking the first steps. Embrace the new opportunities to grow and change course. Where you end up is largely going to be a matter of perspective. Take with you the commitment to always demonstrate that you are a superior parent. Persevere when the path gets steep.

Once you take the initial mental steps that can lead you to where you need to be, it is essential to continue the quest to find the practical knowledge, resources, and guidance that will empower you to better your life, and more importantly, to preserve and enhance your parent-child relationships. The metaphor that I've described, I have lived. Big Rock remains close to my heart; it is now part of who I am.

Without a commitment to my son's well-being, I would never have found Big Rock. I would have missed the high road. Experience has been my guide, but I hope that *this book* can be yours. If you have learned anything through the experiences that I have shared and, if as a result, your children are prevented from shouldering at least some of the unnecessary baggage that they will forever carry, then it has been a worthwhile journey for us both.

When it comes to improving the quality of your children's lives, don't ever despair. Take the high road. It will take you and your children where you want to go.

Resources & Appendices

The pages that follow contain helpful resources as you continue your parenting journey. Sample parenting language and sample parenting clauses may help to guide you and your ex as you move forward. The comprehensive parenting agreement and the collaborative contract are excellent tools to help keep you and your children safe on the high road. The websites, organizations, and books recommended in appendix F have helped me in my journey and I hope they will help you in yours.

A Sample Parenting Language

This document contains some sample language to memorialize the intended plan for separated and divorced parents to continue to live in conformity with certain guiding principles in order to raise happy and emotionally healthy children. These sample clauses are also designed to demonstrate a mutual commitment to minimizing conflict when differences arise (and they will).

Sample Clauses

We both acknowledge that we have been guided by what we believe to be the best interests of John, our precious child. As his parents we affirm our desire to continue to be guided by his best interests in parenting him in the future.

Above all, we want John to know that regardless of the decisions made, these decisions are not to be misinterpreted or in any way diminish the love we have for him. In fact, it is our belief that

John will be afforded a better childhood with us, his parents, living separate and apart from one another. With this in mind, we agree that neither of us shall do anything, nor permit anyone else to do anything, that may estrange John from either of us or injure the opinion or bond that John has or will have regarding us as his parents.

Further, recognizing and believing how important it is for John to grow up knowing that he is a part of each of us, we also agree never to hamper, minimize, or diminish the love that he has for the other parent.

We, John's loving and concerned parents, agree to the following principles of positive parenting:

1. We acknowledge that it is in our son's best interest for both of us, his parents, to continue to participate in the care, rearing, and nurturing of our child and agree that our intent is to encourage the involvement of each other in the care of and responsibilities of raising John into a happy and healthy young adult.

2. We agree to keep each other informed regarding the welfare and circumstances of our child while he is sharing time with either of us and we further agree to permit and encourage communication by the other with school officials, teachers, medical providers, coaches, and officials and other professionals involved with our child.

3. We recognize that parenting is not easy and that John's needs and developmental stages will change as he grows older. Accordingly, our goal is to have a workable framework that will allow our parenting plan to be modified as needed from time to time and to afford appropriate access and involvement

with each parent based upon John's changing needs. The ultimate goal for us is to have a parenting plan that will evolve to provide emotional and financial support for John consistent with his emotional needs, developmental stages, and best interests.

4. We agree to provide each other with John's whereabouts and how to contact him upon request, and we will permit and encourage John to contact the other parent on a regular basis.

We agree to the following decision-making plan:

1. All significant decisions concerning our child, including but not limited to his education, religious training, medical care, sports involvement, and other activities, shall be made jointly by us whenever possible and not by either to the exclusion of the other.

2. In the event that we disagree on a significant decision concerning our child, the following dispute resolution agenda will be employed:

   a. The issue of disagreement is to be clearly identified.

   b. Good faith and reasonable efforts will be encouraged to persuade each other of the appropriateness of our respective positions.

   c. If disagreement persists, we shall each independently identify and consult an expert in the field of mediation or other form of conflict resolution to assist in communicating any differences of opinion and proposals for resolution to the other.

   d. We will each undertake study or self-help resources such

as seminars, books, tapes, and CDs to improve our interpersonal communication and listening skills.

e. Should a disagreement persist, we will employ the services of a professional mediator. We will jointly choose the mediator; or, failing that, the mediator shall be chosen by our respective counsel. The cost of mediation shall be divided equally.

f. If we still cannot resolve issues of significance to either or both of us, we shall contact collaboratively trained attorneys and enter into a collaborative family law participation agreement in order to meet, discuss, and meet and discuss some more until we no longer need to do so.

g. Finally, even though it is our desire to avoid court intervention, if disagreement persists, and if collaborative law practices should not resolve the dispute(s), each party reserves the right to litigate the issue before the appropriate court after withdrawing from the collaborative process.

We will handle matters of transportation, medical care, and the dissemination of information in a fair and reasonable manner by agreeing that:

1. Transportation to and from all periods of physical parenting time shall be provided by both parties. Generally speaking, it will be the responsibility of the parent with whom our child is currently spending time to transport John to the other parent and to events and activities that occur when John is with that particular parent.

2. We each expect to have reasonable phone contact with John when he is in the care of the other parent.

3. We each plan to notify the other in the event of any hospital admission prior to any such admission or non-emergency situations, and we will otherwise notify the other in the event of an emergency or as soon as practical.

4. We shall each be entitled to receive and review all medical, educational, and health records and shall be notified in advance of all regularly scheduled doctor visits. Doctor visits shall include but shall not be limited to physicians, psychiatrists, psychologists, and licensed certified social workers.

5. Both of us shall be listed as contact persons with John's school and either of us may pick him up or drop him off from school.

6. We will attempt to have face-to-face discussions from time to time, or telephone conferences, and/or share e-mails periodically to discuss issues relating to the parenting and support of our child with the goal of fostering positive relationships for the benefit of our child as well as maintaining open lines of communication between ourselves relating to parenting issues.

Preparing to Draft a Settlement Agreement

Depending on the nature of your previous association with your ex and the past co-mingling of life events, when you and the other parent separate or divorce it is easy to forget all of the entanglements that may need to be addressed. Whether you and that other person were involved only briefly enough to have conceived a child or if you have been married for fifteen years with five children and substantial marital assets, it is easy to overlook some of the things that should be addressed.

Whether you are the "leaver" or the "leave-ee," you should review this fairly comprehensive list of topics so that you can make sure that all of your particular issues, needs, and concerns are appropriately addressed. There are generally about fifty or more considerations that should be addressed upon separation.

Think of it like this: fifty ways to leave your lover!

1. Explanatory Statement

This should contain some basic recitals, such as these:

- when and where married; children born to the parties; when separated; and the desire to resolve issues such as:
- living separate and apart from one another, voluntarily and by mutual consent, with the purpose and intent of ending their marriage; issues of parenting; support; maintenance; alimony; respective rights in the property or estate of the other, and in property owned by them; and all other matters of every kind and character arising from their marital relationship and the parenting of their children in common, whether the parties are married or not.

2. Relinquishment of Marital Rights
3. Rights Incident to Marital Relationship and Rights as Surviving Spouse
4. Parenting Plan (See model comprehensive parenting plan in appendix D)
5. Residential Schedule
6. Holidays and Vacations
7. Right of First Refusal
8. Medical and Educational Records and Access to Information
9. Decision-Making Authority
10. Dispute Resolution /Mediation/ Collaborative Law
11. Sports & Extracurricular Activities
12. Summer Camp /Daycare
13. Before and After School Care
14. Transportation
15. Life Insurance
16. Child Support & Related Tax Consequences
17. Medical Insurance and Expenses

18. Extraordinary Expenses
19. Savings Plans
20. College
21. Alimony and Spousal Support
22. Marital Property Generally
23. Personal Property
24. Family Use Property
25. Use & Possession of Family Home
26. Vehicles
27. Auto Insurance
28. Utilities
29. Inheritance
30. Pensions & Retirement Accounts
31. Pension Waiver
32. Real Property/Land
33. Debts
34. Mutual Release and Hold Harmless
35. Subsequent Disputes / Modifications
36. Further Assurances
37. Representation by Independent Counsel
38. Counsel Fees & Court Costs
39. New Relationships & Stepparent Issues
40. Fairness of Terms
41. In the event that one parent dies and custody goes to the other parent, that parent agrees to support in all good faith the relationship between the children and the extended family of the deceased parent including but not limited to reasonable visitation with the extended family.
42. Relocation Issues /Out of State

---

43. Private Schooling

44. Religious Upbringing

45. This Agreement contains the entire understanding between the parties. No modification or waiver of any of the terms of this Agreement will be valid unless made in writing and signed by the parties.

46. Except as allowed by law, the parties agree that no provision of this Agreement will be subject to modification by any Court.

47. Should any provision of this Agreement be found, held, or deemed to be unenforceable, voidable, or void, as contrary to law or public policy under the laws of [YOUR STATE]or any other State of the United States, the parties intend that the remaining provisions of this Agreement will nevertheless continue in full force and effect.

48. As to these covenants and promises, the parties hereto severally bind themselves, their heirs, personal representatives, and assigns.

49. Special Considerations Like Drug and Alcohol Use

50. Witness to Signing the Agreement

Sample Parenting Clauses

C

R eader, some of the clauses in this appendix may seem unnecessary, and perhaps even silly, superfluous, or downright
stupid. I agree. I didn't invent this stuff. Should this be necessary? No; but, if you bought this book, or wish that your children's
other parent had, then it may not be a bad idea to consider adding
some of these clauses into any written agreements that involve the
parenting of your children. Look and see if there are any particular clauses that the other parent would be guilty of having violat-
ed so far. How about you? No, never!

1. **CIVIL TREATMENT:** All conversations, interactions, and deal-
ings of any sort between us shall be conducted in a civil and
courteous manner. (This one is my favorite!)

2. **DISCUSSION WITH CHILDREN:** Neither of us will discuss
the legal aspects of our separation, potential litigation, or

other adult issues with or in front of our children or permit third persons to do so. (Happens all the time!)

3. **NO DISPARAGEMENT:** We will not disparage each other or other family members in front of our children or permit third persons to do so. Our children shall not be encouraged or permitted to call non-parents "mother," "father," or their equivalents. (Happens more than you might think!)

4. **DRUGS, ALCOHOL OR TOBACCO:** Obviously, neither of us will ever be under the influence of alcohol or illegal drugs while our children are in our respective care. (I have had a few clients who have been arrested for DUI with their children in the car during visitation; go figure!)

5. **PROMPT NOTICE:** We will promptly and fully disclose to the other parent any event that affects our children's health, education, behavior, or general welfare. (A frequent and common complaint, usually made by the non-custodial parent — being "left in the dark"!)

6. **APPOINTMENTS:** We will give each other timely notice of our children's medical appointments, school events, parent-teacher meetings, counseling sessions, and the like.

7. **RECORDS:** We are each fully authorized and expected to have complete access to all of our children's educational, medical, or psychological records or any other record or notice that is available to either parent. This includes the right to speak with and obtain information from teachers, counselors, and medical providers. (When it comes to your children's records, it is not the time for "hide and seek" games, is it?)

8. **SCHOOLWORK:** We will preserve all schoolwork, school

projects, report cards, interim reports, disciplinary reports, or anything of like importance sent home from the school for the other parent's periodic review. (Share the credit!)

9. **ADDRESS AND PHONE NUMBERS:** We will keep each other informed of our respective residential addresses, as well as work and home phone numbers. Calls to our places of employment shall not be made, except to discuss important matters concerning our children that cannot wait until the end of the business day or unless we have agreed to accept calls at work. Calls to the residence shall be at reasonable times and intervals. If the children will be staying overnight outside of the local area, we will provide a travel itinerary and contact phone number for the children. (Why? Because that is what normal decent parents do!)

10. **PROMPTNESS:** We agree to be on time and to have the children appropriately ready to go given the specifics of the particular situation. (Try, try, and try some more; teach by providing a good example.)

11. **SCHEDULED ACTIVITIES:** When one of us is exercising parenting time, that person shall be responsible to ensure the attendance of the children at scheduled organized activities such as music or dance lessons, sports practices or games, or regularly attended religious services. We agree not to enroll the minor children in any new organized activities of this type, or commit the children to other activities such as sleepovers or birthday parties that will take place during the other parent's scheduled time without prior consent of the affected party. (This one is often a source of parental contention. Focus on supporting your children in their activities and take

pleasure in watching and participating. Let them be children!)

12. **DISCIPLINE:** We will try hard to have a consistent set of rules of behavior and methods of discipline that apply to our children. Areas of concern include TV time and programming, Internet access, computer and video game use, curfews, bedtimes, and peer associations. (That is a tough enough job when you live under the same roof! Just wait for those teenage years!)

13. **GENERAL WELFARE:** Our children shall be properly supervised at all times and they shall not be exposed to intimate adult activities. The children's regular established meal and bedtime routines shall be adhered to as closely as possible. Any medicine or special diet regimen shall be adhered to. The children should be returned with all special clothing or other personal belongings that should be returned. Homework assignments due for the next school day should be completed. (Makes sense to me! You?)

D

Sample Comprehensive Parenting Agreement

There is no question that the English language is a peculiar animal — you say tomato, I say *tomoto*. It has also been said that the **bold type** giveth and the *fine print* taketh away. When you are drafting a document that has such profound importance and significance in your children's future, it is essential that there be little, if anything, open to interpretation.

While each stage of childhood brings new challenges, experience has demonstrated that usually the parents tend to fight more when the children are of tender years. As children grow older and have more of their own routines, schedules, social engagements, school events, sports, and extracurricular activities, the constant parent versus parent model loses its momentum. When approaching high school, most of the decisions about primary residence, daycare, after school care, medical providers, religious upbringing, and the like have all been settled in one way or another. Most child custody litigators will tell you that it seems like there is often more to fight about when the children are in that preschool age group.

The best course of action is to plan for the worst and hope for the best. In other words, plan out everything that you can conceivably think of and then hope that you and your children's other parent get along well enough that you never even need to look at the written agreement. You need to strive for flexibility in your parenting; but when planning for it, you would be wise to master the art of carefully crafting the letter and spirit of the written directives that will be followed should there be a communication meltdown. What follows here is an illustrative example of a comprehensive parenting agreement.

A Comprehensive Parenting Agreement

It is the mutual desire of the parties in this Agreement to formalize their separation and to settle all questions of custody, visitation, and support (now called child access, parenting time, parental decision-making authority, financial support, and other joint and individual rights and responsibilities) pertaining to their Minor Child. It is the intention of the parties to enter into a separate written Property Settlement Agreement to resolve all other matters of every kind and character arising from their marital relationship, as this document is limited to parenting issues and parent-child and parent-parent relationships.

NOW, THEREFORE, in consideration of the mutual promises of each of the parties, and other good and valuable considerations, the receipt of which each party hereby acknowledges, one to the other, the parties hereby covenant and agree with each other and for their respective heirs, personal representatives, and assigns, as follows:

1. **NOTICE AND ADDRESS.** Until such time as the Minor Child shall attain the age of eighteen (18) years or shall have graduated high school, whichever is last to occur, the parties shall provide their current address and telephone numbers for their residences and promptly provide notice of any changes regarding same to the other party.

2. **CHILD SUPPORT.** The payment of child support for each Minor Child shall terminate upon the first to happen of the following: Attainment of the age of eighteen (18) years by the Child; Marriage of the Child; Death of the Child or the party paying support; provided however, if at the time of termination by reason of age, the child has not yet completed high school, support for said Minor Child shall continue until completion, dismissal, or voluntary termination of high school, but in any event, no later than age twenty (20). Every three (3) years, and/or as either of the parties attain new employment, the parties shall exchange federal and state tax returns and current pay stubs for the purpose of calculating and/or making any adjustments to the child support amount.

3. **PLANS FOR COLLEGE EDUCATION.** Given the fact that the parties have always shared the goal of providing for their child's college education, both parties agree that they will contribute to the cost of college for their child. As of the date of this agreement, the current state-sponsored plan that was set up during the marriage for the benefit of their child will continue to grow untouched, and any money that either party contributes from this time forward shall remain untouched and used exclusively for college with any and all monies from these accounts to be used to pay for the child's

college first, and then any remaining costs would be paid by the parties after evaluating their respective financial situations upon the child entering the last year of high school.

4. **DAYCARE EXPENSES FOR THE MINOR CHILD.** The parties agree to continue the current daycare plans for their child and they agree to split the costs in proportion to the percentages per the Child Support Guidelines. The parties agree that as additional support for the Minor Child, and pursuant to the Child Support Guidelines, any and all daycare expenses for the Minor Child, including before care and after care, shall be paid by the parties as follows: Child's father pays _____% of the daycare expenses and child's mother pays _____% of the daycare expenses. In the event either party should pay a daycare expense to the provider above and/or beyond his/her allocated percentage then the non-paying party agrees to reimburse the other party for their share of the expense upon presentment of a receipt and/or bill for such expense. The reimbursement due shall be paid within ten (10) business days. The daycare costs shall also be paid from child's father to child's mother from the father's employer and deducted from his pay and/or by an Earnings Withholding Order and added to the amount paid to child's mother for the basic child support obligation as expressed in the previous paragraph. However, the actual dollar amount will not be specified in the Order so as to allow for adjustments in daycare expenses and payments without having to obtain a modification of the child support order if and when daycare expenses would change.

5. **INSURANCE AND MEDICAL EXPENSES FOR THE MINOR CHILD.** Each party shall be provided with insurance cards

and similar documentation so that they are fully informed of the coverage available and either parent shall be able to secure any treatment for the child when in their individual care.

6. **UNINSURED MEDICAL EXPENSES.** The parties agree that as additional support for the Minor Child and in consideration of the terms as detailed in this Agreement, the parties shall share (____% Husband - ____% Wife) all uninsured medical, dental, hospital, optometry, orthodontia, child counseling, or similar expenses for the Minor Child above and beyond 250.00 per calendar year. Co-payments incurred while the Minor Child is in the care of either parent shall be the responsibility of that parent to pay at that time, up to $250.00 per calendar year. If either party incurs more than 250.00 per calendar year, any co-pays exceeding that amount will be shared with the child's father paying ___% of costs, and child's mother paying ____% of costs to be paid at the end of the calendar year after an accounting of same is presented to the other party. The reimbursement due shall be paid within ten (10) business days after presentment. The parties agree that they shall use their best efforts to utilize the insurance plan, its provider networks, coverage terms or medical plan participants, for any medical needs of the Minor Child. The obligation to contribute to uninsured medical, dental, hospital, optometry, orthodontia, child counseling, or similar expense for the Child shall terminate upon the first to happen of the following: (a) Attainment of the age of twenty-one (21) years by the Child; (b) Marriage of the Child; (c)

Child becoming fully self-supporting; (d) Death of the Child or the party paying support.

7. **RIGHT OF FIRST REFUSAL.** The parties acknowledge and agree to honor a Right of First Refusal, with the understanding that at any time their child will not be with a parent overnight or for more than a few hours; (outside of daycare or after school care) the other parent shall be offered, without obligation, to spend that time with the child.

8. The parties further agree to notify the other parent of their child's whereabouts and contact information at any time either parent takes the child out of town.

9. The parties acknowledge that the parent providing care for the Minor Child shall be responsible for all transportation and related duties associated with activities scheduled during the time with each parent, such as school events, games, practices, and similar extracurricular activities.

10. Each party shall be entitled to two (2) weeks summer vacation with the Minor Child, uninterrupted from the other parent. The parties agree that the two (2) weeks will be nonconsecutive; unless otherwise agreed to. The parties shall notify one another on or before May 1 of each year as to the weeks they intend to take vacation with the Minor Child. In odd years, child's mother shall have first choice as to which two (2) weeks of vacation she intends to take with the Minor Child. In even years, child's father shall have first choice as to which two (2) weeks of vacation he intends to take with the Minor Child. A week is defined as 7 calendar days. Vacation week schedules cannot interrupt school schedules once the child reaches school age.

11. The vacation schedule shall supersede any conflict over the regular care schedule, but shall not supersede the Holiday schedule, unless expressly agreed to by the parties.

12. **HOLIDAYS.** The parties agree that they shall share in the holidays and school holidays for the Minor Child. The parties agree to the following holiday access schedule:

A. **THANKSGIVING:** In odd years, the Minor Child shall be in the care of the mother on Thanksgiving Day from 9:00 a.m. until 9:00 a.m. Friday morning. In even years, the Minor Child shall be in the care of the father on Thanksgiving Day from 9:00 a.m. until 9:00 a.m. Friday morning.

B. **CHRISTMAS:** In odd years, the father shall have the Minor Child in his care from December 24th beginning at 1:00 p.m. through December 25th at 12:00 p.m. (noon). In odd years, the mother shall have the Minor Child in her care from December 25th beginning at 12:00 p.m. (noon) through December 26th at 8:00 p.m. In even years, the mother shall have the Minor Child in her care from December 24th beginning at 1:00 p.m. through December 25th at 12:00 p.m. (noon). In even years, the father shall have the Minor Child in his care from December 25th beginning at 12:00 p.m. (noon) through December 26th at 8:00 p.m.

C. **EASTER:** In even years, the mother shall have the Minor Child in her care from 5:00 p.m. Saturday before Easter until 5:00 p.m. Easter Sunday. In odd years, the father shall have the Minor Child in his care from 5:00 p.m. Saturday before Easter until 5:00 p.m. Easter Sunday.

D. **FATHER'S AND MOTHER'S DAY:** The Minor Child shall be in the care of the father on Father's Day and in the care of the mother on Mother's Day. This will be from 5:00 p.m. the Saturday before the holiday to 5:00 p.m. on the Sunday of the holiday.

E. **ALTERNATING SCHEDULE:** The following additional holidays shall be celebrated with the Minor Child in the care of the parties (alternating year schedule) as follows:

- **MEMORIAL DAY** (Mother in odd years; Father in even years)
- **FOURTH OF JULY** (Father in odd years; Mother in even years)
- **LABOR DAY** (Mother in odd years; Father in even years)
- **HALLOWEEN** (Mother in even years; Father in odd years)

F. Except as specifically provided for by the terms and provisions of this Agreement, the parties shall share all other school recesses (excluding summer break from school) which may exist on the school calendar for the Minor Child either by an equal division or alternating of same between the parties.

G. The child's mother and the child's father shall alternate the birthday celebrations for the Minor Child each year. The alternating schedule shall begin with mother coordinating/hosting the birthday celebrations in 20__.

H. Unless otherwise detailed in this Agreement, the parties shall have the Minor Child during the aforementioned holidays from 5:00 p.m. the night before overnight to 5:00 p.m. on the holiday.

    I. The holiday schedule shall supercede any conflict over the regular care schedule.

13. **CHILD RELATED DECISION-MAKING PROCEDURE & JOINT LEGAL CUSTODY.** The parties shall consult with each other in a meaningful manner on the matters of health, education, and religious upbringing, and other significant matters relating to the welfare and well-being of the Minor Child. The parties agree that the child's current medical providers are acceptable to both parties and that the daycare providers are acceptable to both parties. The parties agree to continue participation in the child's current extracurricular activities. In addition, the parties anticipate that their child will attend Happy Orchard for Kindergarten beginning in the fall of 20___. The parties further agree that the child will attend school in the mother's school district. Notwithstanding the above agreements, the parties currently do not believe that joint custody will work beyond what is agreed to herein, however, both parties are willing to try to make decisions in that fashion. However, if in the future the parties do not agree on any other significant decisions, after full and meaningful discussion and an opportunity to attend mediation, and/or proceed by the collaborative family law model, they reserve the right to have this limited issue (final decision-making authority) decided by the court at a later date. Similarly, the parties agree to continue with the child's current activities and they further agree to discuss enrolling the child in any other activities that would encroach upon the scheduled time

of either parent with the minor child. If they are unable to resolve such issues without resorting to litigation, the parties agree that such action will be evidence of their inability to make joint decisions and they will ask the court to grant one or the other final decision-making authority on that issue and for all such future parental decisions.

14. Neither party shall do or say anything which may estrange the Minor Child from the other parent or injure the opinion held by the Minor Child with regard to each parent. With regard to their communications and decision-making procedures, the parties agree to communicate with each other regarding the Minor Child in a civil manner, respecting each other's interests in their welfare. The parties agree that all discussions will be between the two of them and they will avoid using the Minor Child as a means of communication. Both parties will encourage contact with each parent. Neither party shall question their Minor Child about a parent's activities or attempt to elicit such information.

15. Each party shall be entitled to medical or educational information relating to their Minor Child. To the extent possible and practical, each parent shall be kept fully informed of medical and dental appointments, games and practices, and school conferences. Copies of report cards shall be provided promptly to each parent.

16. Each party shall be entitled to access to the Minor Child's medical or health care providers, school teachers, officials, tutors and activity leaders. Each party shall be entitled to medical, educational, or similar information and/or records relating to the general welfare, well-being, and activities of

the Minor Child. Each party shall execute and deliver any authorization so that information concerning the Minor Child shall be equally available to both parties.

17. Each party shall be entitled to reasonable telephone access and communication with each of the Minor Child while in the care of the other parent.

18. Neither party shall make a decision without the opportunity for meaningful consultation and joint decision-making regarding the health, education, religious training, residency and other issues significantly affecting the welfare of the Minor Child.

19. **FURTHER ASSURANCES.** The parties, for themselves and for their respective heirs, personal representatives, and assigns, do mutually agree to join in or execute any instruments and to do any other act or thing which may be necessary to carry into effect any of the provisions of this Agreement.

20. **COMPLETE AGREEMENT/MODIFICATIONS IN WRITING.** The parties acknowledge that there have been no representations, warranties, assurances, promises, or covenants made by either party as an inducement to enter into this Agreement, other than those set forth herein, and that this Agreement contains all of the terms and agreements of the parties. The parties further agree that in the event they shall at any future time resume living together that the interruption of their separation will not however act to terminate the provisions of this Agreement.

21. **INCORPORATION IN DECREE.** This Agreement is not intended in any way to affect or prejudice the rights of either

party to bring suit for divorce. This Agreement shall survive and continue in full force whether or not a judgment of divorce shall be entered in any action between the parties in any jurisdiction. In case a judgment of divorce shall be entered in any jurisdiction in favor of either party, the terms of this Agreement shall, at the request of either party, be incorporated but not merged in the judgment of the court to the extent possible.

22. **REPRESENTATION BY COUNSEL.** The parties acknowledge that Husband has been represented by Dewy, Cheetom and Howe, P.C. Wife acknowledges that she has not relied upon any advice, recommendation, or counsel from Husband's separate counsel or any advice provided by Husband. The parties acknowledge that Wife has been represented by Ben Dover, Esquire. Husband acknowledges that he has not relied upon any advice or recommendation from Wife's separate counsel or any advice provided by Wife. Each party acknowledges that they fully understand the terms and provisions of this Agreement and has signed this Agreement freely and voluntarily. Neither party shall be deemed the drafter of this Agreement as it contains the terms and provisions which each of them desire after consideration of all available resolutions whether mediation, litigation, or negotiation.

23. **FAIRNESS OF TERMS.** Each party fully understands the facts and has been fully informed as to his or her legal rights and obligations and, having had such advice, and with such knowledge, each of them is signing this Agreement freely and voluntarily and each party believes this Agreement to

be fair, just, and reasonable and in the best interests of their Minor Child.

24. **BREACH OF AGREEMENT.** If either party hereto fails or refuses to act with the utmost good faith and due diligence to carry out each and every term and condition of this Agreement, and after fifteen (15) days written notice and opportunity to comply, the offending party still refuses to act with the utmost good faith and due diligence to carry out his or her responsibilities as set forth herein, and in the event the innocent party seeks the assistance of any court to compel the offending party to comply with his or her responsibilities as set forth herein, then and in that event, the offending party shall be responsible for all reasonable attorneys' fees, expenses and court costs actually incurred by the innocent party upon a finding by that court that the offending party was without substantial justification for failing to act in the utmost good faith and due diligence in carrying out the terms and conditions of this Agreement which forms the basis for the innocent party's complaint.

25. **ENTIRE AGREEMENT.** There have been no representations, terms, conditions, statements, warranties, promises, covenants or understandings, oral or written, other than those expressly set forth herein.

26. **SEVERABILITY.** In case any provision (or any part of any provision) contained in this Agreement shall for any reason be held to be invalid, illegal or unenforceable in any respect, such invalidity, illegality or unenforceability shall not affect any other provision (or remaining part of the affected provision) of this Agreement but this Agreement shall be con-

strued as if such invalid, illegal, or unenforceable provision (or part thereof) had never been contained herein but only to the extent it is invalid, illegal, or unenforceable.

27. **GOVERNING LAW.** The parties agree that the terms and provisions of this Agreement shall be interpreted under the laws of this state.

28. **AGREEMENT BINDING.** This Agreement shall be binding upon the parties hereto, their heirs, personal representatives, and assigns.

See the following two pages for the sample signature pages for this Sample Comprehensive Parenting Agreement.

AS WITNESS the hands and seals of the parties the day and year first above written.

_____ (Father)

and

_____ (Mother)

```
┌──────────────┐
│              │
│    (SEAL)    │
│              │
└──────────────┘

┌──────────────┐
│              │
│    (SEAL)    │
│              │
└──────────────┘
```

OUR STATE, OUR COUNTY, to wit:

I HEREBY CERTIFY that on this _____ day of _____ , 20_____, before me, the subscriber, a Notary Public of this State and County aforesaid, personally appeared _____ (Mother) and she made oath in due form of law that the matters and facts set forth in the foregoing Agreement with respect to the separation of the parties and all other matters stated herein are true and correct as therein stated and acknowledged said Agreement to be her act.

AS WITNESS my hand and Notarial Seal.

NOTARY PUBLIC

My Commission Expires: _____

```
┌──────────────┐
│              │
│    (SEAL)    │
│              │
└──────────────┘
```

I HEREBY CERTIFY that on this _____ day of _____ , 20_____ , before me, the subscriber, a Notary Public of this State and County aforesaid, personally appeared _____ (Father) and he made oath in due form of law that the matters and facts set forth in the foregoing Agreement with respect to the separation of the parties and all other matters stated herein are true and correct as therein stated and acknowledged said Agreement to be his act.

AS WITNESS my hand and Notarial Seal.

NOTARY PUBLIC

(SEAL)

My Commission Expires: _____

The Collaborative Contract

E

Collaborative Participation Agreement

L ooking at this model participation agreement, it is hard to imagine choosing litigation over collaboration. Isn't this the way parents should act when they have differences to work out, especially when it concerns the welfare of their children? In the past, litigation has been the road most traveled, but collaborative participation is a much safer path — safer for you and safer for your children. Use this sample agreement as your guide and stay on the high road.

PARTICIPATION AGREEMENT

Between

_____ ("Husband")
Represented by Jane B. Fairshake, Esquire

and

_____ ("Wife")
Represented by William Ben Evolent, Esquire

I. GOALS

A. Husband and Wife wish to resolve their differences in the Collaborative Process ("Collaboration") instead of going to court.

B. Husband and Wife and both Attorneys agree to:

1. focus on the future well-being of Husband and Wife and their children;

2. resolve all of Husband's and Wife's differences in the best interests of their children and each other;

3. promote a caring, loving, and involved relationship between the children and their parents;

4. keep the children out of their differences;

5. act quickly to resolve differences related to Husband's and Wife's children;

6. find solutions that are acceptable to Husband and Wife; and

7. try to reduce the negative emotional, social, and fi-

nancial consequences of Husband's and Wife's separation.

8. conclude all matters necessary so that a written Separation and Property Settlement Agreement dealing with all issues of property, support, custody, visitation and other issues will be executed by both parties.

II. ROLE OF ATTORNEYS

A. The Attorneys will work together with Husband and Wife to help them:
   1. discover what is important to each of them;
   2. identify the questions the clients need to answer;
   3. gather information;
   4. create the maximum number of options which may help the clients meet their goals; and
   5. reach a comprehensive agreement.

B. The Husband and Wife will give complete, honest, and open disclosure of all information. They will ask for and provide information only in the four-way Collaboration meetings, except as agreed upon between professionals and Husband and Wife.

C. The Attorneys may discuss the likely outcome of going to court. Neither Attorney will use threats of court as a way to force settlement.

D. The Attorneys may file an uncontested divorce or other consent court documents reflecting the terms of Husband's and Wife's agreements reached in Collaboration.

III. PARTICIPATION WITH INTEGRITY

A. Husband, Wife, and the Attorneys will act in good faith with:
1. respect;
2. honesty;
3. openness;
4. cooperation; and
5. moderation.

B. Husband, Wife, and the Attorneys will work to protect the privacy and dignity of everyone participating in this Collaboration.

C. All participants in Collaboration understand that the success of Collaboration depends on the participants' commitment to working hard together.

D. When Husband's and Wife's priorities, hopes, and goals differ, all four participants will use their best efforts to create proposals that are acceptable to Husband and Wife. If necessary, Husband and Wife will compromise to reach an acceptable agreement.

E. Each participant will immediately identify and correct any mistakes. No one will take advantage of any mistakes made by anyone in Collaboration.

IV. NEUTRAL CONSULTANTS

A. If Husband and Wife need Neutral Consultants, they will retain them jointly.

B. All Neutral Consultants will be requested to be neutral and to assist Husband and Wife to resolve their differences without going to court.

C. A Neutral Consultant may be asked to provide additional information and recommendations related to the children. After considering such additional information or recommendations, Husband and Wife together will make their own decisions about what is best for their children.

D. When Husband and Wife retain Neutral Consultants, they agree that the Attorneys and the Neutral Consultants may have whatever discussions among themselves as are necessary to assist Husband and Wife in resolving their differences during Collaboration.

V. DIVORCE COACHES

A. Husband or Wife may decide that he or she will use a Divorce Coach. They may use a joint Divorce Coach if appropriate.

B. If Husband or Wife retains a Divorce Coach individually or jointly, he or she agrees that the Divorce Coach, the Attorneys, and the Neutral Consultants may have whatever discussions among themselves as are necessary to assist Husband and Wife in resolving their differences during Collaboration.

VI. CAUTIONS

A. Husband and Wife understand that Collaboration is designed to solve only their legal problems arising from their separation. Collaboration is not personal or marriage counseling.

B. Husband and Wife understand there is no guarantee that

they will successfully resolve their differences with Collaboration.

C. Husband and Wife understand and agree that each Attorney and each Divorce Coach represents only his or her own client in Collaboration, even though all participants will work together.

D. No formal discovery procedure, as set forth in our State's Family Law Article, or our State's Rules of Procedure, will be used during Collaboration unless specifically agreed to in writing by Husband, Wife, and their Attorneys. Husband and Wife acknowledge that by using informal discovery, they surrender certain fact-finding procedures and methods available in litigation. If Collaboration fails and Husband and Wife resort to litigation, they agree that participation in Collaboration does not waive their rights to all discovery devices provided for by the State Family Law Rules. Although not restricted by the requirements of formal discovery, Husband and Wife expressly agree to make full and fair disclosure of all assets, incomes, debts, expenses, and all other information necessary for a principled and complete settlement. Participation in Collaboration is grounded on the assumption that Husband and Wife will act in good faith and provide complete and accurate information to the best of their ability. From time to time, Husband and Wife shall be required to sign financial statements substantially in the form required by the State's Rules of Civil Procedure, making full and fair disclosure of their incomes, expenses, assets, and liabilities. Such statements will be signed with the following affirmation: "I hereby declare under the penalties of perjury the foregoing is true, accurate, and complete to the best of my current knowledge, information and belief."

E. All participants understand that Collaboration may not be successful in all situations and for all participants for reasons such as:

1. Husband or Wife not following the list of Expectations of Clients and Professionals during collaborative meetings (attached to this Contract as Schedule "A");

2. Husband or Wife not following the Expectations of Clients and Professionals in conversations with each other *outside* Collaboration;

3. Husband or Wife not following temporary agreements they make in Collaboration;

4. Husband or Wife not performing tasks they have agreed to do in Collaboration; or

5. Husband or Wife taking one-sided actions during Collaboration.

F. Husband and Wife understand that both Attorneys must withdraw from Collaboration if either learns that Husband or Wife has taken unfair advantage of Collaboration. Some examples include, but are not limited to:

1. taking serious, one-sided actions;

2. disposing of property without the consent of the other person;

3. withholding or misrepresenting information;

4. failing to disclose the existence or the true nature of assets or liabilities;

---

5. failing to follow agreements made in Collaboration; or

6. failing in any other way to participate in the spirit of Collaboration or the terms of this Contract. This includes, but is not limited to, seeking advice of a litigation attorney while the Husband and Wife are in this process.

G. If either Husband's Attorney or Wife's Attorney withdraws from Collaboration, that Attorney will give written notice of the withdrawal to his or her own client, the other Attorney, the Divorce Coaches, and any Neutral Consultants.

VII. LEGAL FEES AND COSTS

A. Husband has retained Husband's Attorney and will pay Husband's Attorney for Husband's Attorney's legal services.

B. Wife has retained Wife's Attorney and will pay Wife's Attorney for Wife's Attorney's legal services.

VIII. FEES AND COSTS FOR DIVORCE COACHES AND NEUTRAL CONSULTANTS

A. If Husband and Wife retain Divorce Coaches, they will decide in Collaboration how they will pay the Divorce Coach.

B. If Husband and Wife retain a Neutral Consultant, they will decide in Collaboration how they will pay the Neutral Consultant.

IX. PROCEDURES IF HUSBAND OR WIFE CHOOSES TO GO TO COURT

A. Husband and Wife understand that his or her Attorney's representation is limited to Collaboration. Neither Husband's Attorney nor Wife's Attorney can ever represent either client in a contested court proceeding against the other client.

B. Husband and Wife understand that his or her Divorce Coach's representation is limited to Collaboration (until the Divorce Coach is permitted to take on another role by the regulations of that Divorce Coach's professional governing body).

C. If Collaboration ends and Husband and Wife go to court, all Neutral Consultants will be disqualified as witnesses. Except as otherwise provided herein, any written material in the Neutral Consultants' files, opinions, and reports will be inadmissible as evidence, unless Husband and Wife and the Neutral Consultants agree otherwise in writing. Notwithstanding the terms of the preceding sentence, "Agreements Husband and Wife Can Rely On" are agreements between Husband and Wife made during Collaboration and identified in the written Minutes from Collaboration. Such Agreements may be admissible in court.

D. If either Husband or Wife withdraws from Collaboration or files any document in court, he or she must give the other party and both Attorneys written notice of his or her withdrawal from Collaboration. Husband and Wife must not do anything in the court system until thirty (30) days after the delivery of such notices.

E. Notwithstanding the terms of Subparagraph D, above, if either Husband or Wife satisfies a court that there is an emergency requiring immediate action before the thirty (30)-day period expires, then such court action will not be a breach of this Contract.

X. Promise to Follow Contract

A. Husband's Attorney, Wife's Attorney, Husband, and Wife agree to follow this Contract and to promote both the spirit and the written word of this Contract.

This Collaborative Contract is agreed upon by the four (4) parties thereto as indicated by their signatures below on this _____ day of _____, 20_____.

_____ ("Husband")
Represented by Jane B. Fairshake, Esquire

and

_____ ("Wife")
Represented by William Ben Evolent, Esquire

(See following pages for Schedule "A")

SCHEDULE "A"
Expectations of Clients and Professionals

1. Be respectful of everyone in the meeting.
2. Address the problems and concerns at hand. Do not blame or insult each other.
3. Speak for yourself. Make "I" statements.
4. Listen carefully and try to understand what the other person is saying, without judging the person or the message.
5. Use first names for each other and both Attorneys. Avoid "he" or "she."
6. Express yourself in terms of what is important to you, what your concerns are, and what you want to talk about. Avoid positions, black-and-white thinking, and rigidity.
7. Be ready to work for what you believe is the most constructive and acceptable agreement for both you and your family.
8. Do not interrupt when another person is speaking. You will have a full and equal opportunity to speak about everything that is important to you.
9. If you have a complaint, raise it as your concern and follow it up with a constructive suggestion about how it might be resolved.
10. If something is not working for you, please tell your Attorney so that your concern can be addressed. Talk with your Attorney about anything you do not understand. Your Attorney can clarify matters for you.
11. Be willing to commit time to meet regularly.
12. Be prepared for each meeting.

---

13. Be patient with each other and with your Attorneys. Delays in Collaboration can happen, even when everyone is acting in good faith.
14. Remain positive and optimistic about the likelihood of a satisfactory settlement.

Helpful Resources

F

B y the beginning of 1995, I'd completely immersed myself
in a search for knowledge and information to assist me in
surviving my own gut-wrenching divorce and child custody battle (which, by the way, lasted into the turn of the century). Fortunately, you can benefit from that quest. I have done the
majority of the work for you in sifting though thousands of pages
of information from court cases, laws, statutes, books, tapes, meetings, seminars, websites, and organizations that address the issues
I've tackled in this book. While there are countless volumes of information on each topic, I assure you that each of these resources
has been invaluable to me along my path to Big Rock. Some I used
during my divorce and custody battle, and others I've used more
recently on my continuing quest for self-improvement and in continually and effectively assisting parents in conflict. Each resource

meets my personal and professional "stamp of approval." Read, look, listen, and learn. You (and your kids) will be happy you did.

Divorce Resources

Books

The Collaborative Way to Divorce: The Revolutionary Method That Results in Less Stress, Lower Costs, and Happier Kids—Without Going to Court by Stuart G. Webb and Ronald D. Ousky

> This book provides the background of the Collaborative Law movement from its inception. It is the basic who, what, when, where, why, and how as taught by the pioneers of collaborative law.

Collaborative Divorce: The Revolutionary New Way to Restructure Your Family, Resolve Legal Issues, and Move on With Your Life by Pauline H. Tesler and Peggy Thompson

> This book takes collaborative law concepts and principles and provides the mechanics of getting it done correctly. It is replete with real-life examples and helpful illustrations. The authors do a wonderful job of explaining the "team approach" to avoiding court and demonstrate how all sorts of family related issues can be resolved with assistance from neutral financial planers, divorce coaches, therapists, parent coordinators, and the like.

Joint Custody with a Jerk: Raising a Child with an Uncooperative Ex by Julie A. Ross

> The title says it all. This is an outstanding book on improving the communication skills of your ex by helping to reshape

and redefine how you act, react, and interact with your ex. The authors take you through the steps, techniques, and thought processes that form the foundation to effectively deal with a jerk (the other parent). They go into great detail and provide clear and concise models with step-by-step instructions to resolve all sorts of problematic areas of co-parenting. By following the advice provided, you too may avoid acting like a jerk when you otherwise just might. Don't just read it; study it and master the techniques.

Divorce Poison: Protecting the Parent-Child Bond from a Vindictive Ex
by Dr. Richard A. Warshak
After reading this book you will not only know how to recognize child divorce poisoning, you will know what to do about it. A must read if your children are being turned against you.

Fathers' Rights: Hard-Hitting & Fair Advice for Every Father Involved in a Custody Dispute
by Jeffery Leving and Ken Dachman
Jeffrey M. Leving is known as America's Fathers' Rights attorney. In 1998, from a different personal perspective, I wrote to Mr. Leving and complimented him on his search for justice. This is an awesome book and demonstrates the horrors of custody litigation. Whether male or female, if you think that you will be forced to litigate, you had better read this book first.

Ex-Etiquette for Parents: Good Behavior After a Divorce or Separation
by Jann Blackstone-Ford and Sharyl Jupe
This is a great book for parents who've moved beyond fight-

ing but who could use some fine-tuning with the many helpful suggestions on how to turn workable relationships into much better ones, based on a child-focused approach. This is a great book for you to consult to keep your children happy and healthy when you or your ex are involved in new relationships.

Websites

www.collaborativepractice.com

This is the website for the International Academy of Collaborative Professionals. It is the best collaborative law resource available. The IACP is an international community of legal, mental health, and financial professionals working in concert to create client-centered processes for resolving conflict. This organization is committed to fostering professional excellence in conflict resolution through Collaborative Practice and serves as a central resource for education, networking, and standards of practice.

www.cdadivorce.com

Resources and info about collaborative divorce, including links to other sites.

www.CRCkids.org

Website of the Children's Right's Council. Their motto is: "The best parent is both parents."

www.divorcesource.com

A clearinghouse for information and services.

www.DivorceWithoutDishonor.com

This is the home of my blog that is affiliated with
www.MiketheLawyer.com. DWD offers links, articles, and a
host of topics that will appeal to anyone who desires to put
their children first. In addition to being a great resource of information and contacts, it is also intended to be an inspirational place to visit as well as an interactive forum for those
who wish to contribute to a kinder, gentler approach to divorce. It is all about raising children of separation and divorce
into happy and emotionally healthy adults.

www.family-affairs.org

The website of Family Matters™. This organization provides
court -approved online parenting classes for separating, divorcing, and remarrying families in transition.

www.lawtsf.com

Information on collaborative law (don't be dissuaded by the
intro) and links to other websites and resources.

www.slovinlaw.com

More information on collaborative law and other tips for divorcing parents.

www.collaborativetrainingsolutions.com

"Advancing the Collaborative Vision" is their motto and
offering excellent training for collaborative professionals is
what they do.

Organizations

Children's Rights Council

The Children's Rights Council is an internationally recognized leader serving divorced, never married, and extended families and at risk youth for more than twenty years. Headquartered in Landover, Maryland, this organization's motto is: "The best parent is both parents.®" CRC works to ensure children have the frequent, meaningful, and continuing contact with two parents and extended family the children would normally have during a marriage. They work to strengthen families through education, favoring family formation and family preservation. Unlike many of the organizations with some of the same ideals, CRC is genderless. They are neither a woman's group nor a men's group. They advocate what they believe to be in the best interest of children. CRC also operates forty child access Centers (Safe Havens) throughout thirteen states and Washington D.C. to provide neutral drop-off and pick-up of children and supervised access (visitation).

The national organization coordinates state chapters, publishes a quarterly newsletter, testifies on behalf of its positions before the U.S. Congress, communicates with the national media, provides published materials including books, briefs, and cassettes consistent with its purposes, meets with policy makers throughout the country and generally educates people on the plight of our children due to prevalent practices in our courts and departments of human services.

The CRC state chapters vary in breadth and depth of their activities, but essentially act on behalf of children in the same manner as the national organization. Visit their website at www.CRCkids.org.

DivorceCare

DivorceCare groups meet weekly to help you face the challenges of separation and divorce and move toward rebuilding your life. Each DivorceCare session has two distinct elements: a "Seminar with Experts" and a "Support Group with Focus." The first thirty or forty minutes of the meetings, the participants watch a video seminar featuring top experts on divorce and recovery subjects. These videos feature expert interviews and real-life case studies. After viewing the video, the participants spend time as a support group, discussing what was presented in that week's video seminar as well as what is going on in their lives. Visit their website for more information: www.divorcecare.com.

Family Matters

The organization known as Family Matters offers online courses called Parents Forever™ Education for Families in Divorce Transition classes. Parents Forever™ is a parenting program for adults who are divorcing and other situations involving custody of children. While the main office is located in Corpus Christi, Texas, there is no reason to leave the privacy of your home to take advantage of the online programs and resources they have to offer. They provide certificates of completion that are often required when parents are court-ordered to participate in parenting programs. The program is research-based and it is designed and tested by educators at the University of Minnesota. Their programs and courses help:

⮞ Eliminate parental conflicts in the presence of the child

⮞ Keep the child out of the parental issues

⮞ Provide access to both parents

⮞ Put the best interest of the child first

⮞ Find reputable child-focused and solution-oriented books, tapes, and resources

To check it out or to register for any of their courses, visit their website at www.family-affairs.org

The National Family Resiliency Center

The National Family Resiliency Center is an award-winning center with nationally recognized experts and resources who handle a broad scope of family issues. Formerly known as Children of Separation and Divorce (COSD), the organization changed its name to better reflect the impact of these family issues, with an expanded mission to serve. The dedicated professionals at The National Family Resiliency Center, Inc., have made a huge difference in how families, judges, attorneys, and other professionals handle divorce. Most importantly, they have had profound positive influences on the people that they serve.

For over a quarter of a century the center has helped tens of thousands of family members through times of transition and crisis. From premarital counseling to programs for step-families to peer support groups, including KidShare and Teen-Share education programs, the center strives to meet the needs of individuals and families.

The National Family Resiliency Center educates parents about the ages and stages of development of children as it pertains to effectively addressing their issues resulting from the breakup of their parents. I highly recommend that you visit their website at www.divorceABC.com

In addition, NFRC has implemented Family Connex™, an Internet-based program that teaches parents the information needed to create child-focused parent agreements. The self-paced program includes a comprehensive thirty-five-page manual and helpful tools to assist parents in designing a parenting plan. Parents and professionals may access information about this program at http://www.familyconnex.org.

Parenting Resources

Books

1 2 3 Magic: Training Your Children to Do What You Want
by Thomas Phelan

This book is largely about behavior modification techniques that can be effectively utilized on children from the ages of two to twelve. This is a humorous book with easy-to-follow steps that do not include yelling, arguing, or spanking your children to get them to do what you want. It really works!

Get Out of My Life: But First Could You Drive Me and Cheryl to the Mall? A Parent's Guide to the New Teenager
by Anthony E. Wolf, Ph.D. (Revised and updated)

If you have ever thought that some alien came down and stole your lovable, polite, and fun child and replaced him with a teenaged monster, you need to read this book. Teens today get away with things we never could have imagined doing as children — from talking back to calling the shots.

This book explains how that happened and what we can do about it. It shows you how to still raise happy, healthy, respectful, and responsible adults who will love you as you love them when it appears that all hope is lost.

The Golden Rule of Parenting: Using Discipline Wisely
by Phil E. Quinn

An amazing man with scars of an abusive childhood teaches successful parenting techniques with principles based in mutual respect, honesty, love, and acceptance. Quinn discusses developing and fostering effective parent-child relationships by adhering to certain belief and value systems in parenting. The importance of taking care of yourself, understanding basic human behavior, and seeking help when necessary to parent with love and respect are addressed in an easy-to-follow format. I met Dr. Quinn in April of 1995 at a seminar where he taught the principles contained in this book. He believes that children tend to honor their father and mother as they are honored and therefore stresses teaching by example.

Men are From Mars, Women are from Venus... Children are From Heaven
by John Gray, Ph.D.

Gray suggests that we teach our children again and again that it's okay to be different, it's okay to make mistakes, it's okay to express negative emotions, it's okay to want more, and it's okay to say no — but remember mom and dad are the bosses. Let the relationship master show you how to raise cooperative, confident, and compassionate children.

Parenting with Love and Logic
by Foster W. Cline and Jim Fay

With the help of this book, you can learn to become a "Love and Logic" parent — one who empathizes with their children while teaching them responsibility and teaching them how to solve their own problems. This is a great book full of practical examples. Prepare your kids for coping with real-life situations and real-world living.

Websites

www.family.org/parenting

Tips and information about raising children through all the stages, including important topics such as discipline, schooling, sibling rivalry, and bullying.

www.loveandlogic.com

This website doesn't have much information but you can access all of Love and Logic's wonderful parenting resources here. Lots of wonderful titles, including *Love and Logic Magic for Early Childhood: Parenting from Birth to Six Years*, and *Love and Logic Magic: When Kids Leave You Speechless* (if you're dealing with a lot of behavior problems).

Organizations

Parents Without Partners

Parents Without Partners was founded in 1957 in New York City by two single parents who felt isolated from society because of their marital status; they decided to form a mutual support organization. Following their first newspaper advertisements directed to "Parents Without Partners," twenty-five single parents attended the first meeting in a Greenwich Village church basement. Later, media attention brought inquiries from all over the country. Parents Without Partners, Inc., is now the largest international, nonprofit membership organization devoted to the welfare and interests of single parents and their children. Single parents may join one of approximately two hundred chapters. All single parents are welcome — male or female, custodial or noncustodial, separated, divorced, or widowed. The organization provides opportunities for single parents to make friends, receive support, exchange parenting techniques, and enhance their personal growth.

The Empowerment Zone

Books

The 4-Hour Workweek
by Timothy Ferriss

> If one of your goals in life is to have sufficient time and money to watch and enjoy your children as they live and leave childhood, you must read this book. While it may be hard to imagine right now, soon enough, when the dust settles, you may want to consider whether you too can escape the 9-5 daily grind, travel anywhere, and join the new rich. See www.fourhourworkweek.com.

Eat That Frog! 21 Great Ways to Stop Procrastinating and Get More Done in Less Time
By Brian Tracy

Get more done in less time! Tracy's book is the result of over thirty years of studying time management, personal efficiency, and effectiveness. He is one of the best in the business. By learning his methods and techniques and applying them over and over until they become habits, you will alter the course of your life in a very positive way.

The Power of Focus
by Jack Canfield, Mark Victor Hansen, and Les Hewitt

This book put me back on track many times. This essential reading will help you accurately assess where you are and inspire you to develop a plan to get you where you want to be. Clear and concise instructions for a better life. While not about divorce or parenting, it will get you in success mode. If you are going to get through all this divorce and custody nonsense, you better learn to focus. Define your path and start working your plan by learning from the best of the best. Just do it.

The Secret
by Rhonda Byrne

There has recently been a lot of talk about *The Secret*; it's even made it to Oprah. The Secret is a law of attraction. The idea is that the things that are coming into your life, you are attracting into your life. It has a lot to do with images that you hold in your mind. Whatever is most in your mind is what you are attracted to. Thoughts become things. Every thought has a frequency. While no one to my knowledge has presented *The Secret* in terms of custody and visitation disputes, it certainly fits well. You need to focus all of your time, energy, and ambition on positive parenting issues. By doing so you will attract the answers because you will be asking the right questions. See www.thesecret.tv/html.

Self Matters: Creating Your Life from the Inside Out
by Phillip C. McGraw, Ph.D. (Dr. Phil)
When you look in the mirror, who do you see? Now would be a good time to regroup and examine your authentic self. Let's face it, we could all use a good dose of Dr. Phil!

Spiritual Divorce: Divorce as a Catalyst for an Extraordinary Life
by Debbie Ford
A great book for finding a purpose from your pain by seeing your ex-partner as a teacher rather than an enemy. This book will show you how to use your heartache as a catalyst to reinvent yourself, re-create your life, and become the person you have always wanted to be.

Websites

www.landmarkforum.com
The Landmark Forum is specifically designed to bring about positive and permanent shifts in the quality of your life. These shifts are the direct cause for a new and unique kind of freedom and power. I strongly recommend attending their weekend program. Look for changes in the quality of your rela-

tionships and your level of personal productivity. Experience the difference you can make while enjoying your life.

www.thinkrightnow.com

A source for self-improvement programs.

www.beliefnet.com

Everything you could want if you're looking for spirituality, inspiration, and faith. The daily inspirational quotes are usually right on time!

www.drphil.com

"How's that working for you?" Visit this site for some inspiration to overcome ongoing problems.

www.oprah.com

It's Oprah, what could be better? Lots of resources for self-improvement here.

www.drwaynedyer.com

Wayne W. Dyer, Ph.D., is an internationally renowned author and speaker in the field of self-development and affectionally called the "father of motivation" by his fans.

www.debbieford.com

Debbie Ford is a New York Times best-selling author with a mission to help people forgive themselves for their shortcomings, make peace with their humanity. and open themselves to be guided by a higher power.

www.zukav.com
This site explores the world of spirituality and relationships.

Index

Legal Disclaimers

No non-fiction book written by an attorney would be complete without a few disclaimers. Here they are:

1. Every divorce case or child custody dispute is unique, requiring the advice of those versed in the law and legal procedures in your local jurisdiction.
2. Different states have different laws and you should not rely on any information contained herein as a restatement of applicable law as it may pertain to the facts and circumstances of your particular case.
3. While you may or may not like lawyers, you had better consult a few good ones if your access to and involvement with your minor children is at risk.

4. No part of this book is intended to serve as legal advice *per se* and by virtue of your reading any portions thereof, no attorney-client relationship is formed, implied, or intended.

5. While many of the thoughts and materials presented in this book are based upon my personal and professional experiences, I did not develop many of the ideas and principles and I do not intend to pass off the works of others as my own. Having said that, when I went through my own gut-wrenching divorce and child custody battle, I became what I have called a "student of positive parenting." In so doing, I desired to learn all that I could about things that I felt were relevant to separation, divorce, and child custody disputes while raising a child during times of extreme parental conflict.

6. Some articles can be traced to their original authors, and others cannot. I have compiled useful information from a huge number of sources and I have endeavoured to package it for you in the context of preserving parent-child relationships through contested child custody and divorce situations with the added benefit of my twenty years of personal and professional experiences.

7. If I have borrowed from sources that have not been appropriately identified or credited, I am sorry, but grateful, for those worthy contributions. As comedian Steven Wright said, "To steal ideas from one person is plagiarism: to steal ideas from many is research." He probably heard it someplace else first.

Thank You

Deb, our guardian angel, my wonderful wife, and my best friend. Thank you for turning our house into a home and restoring family values to our lives. I am eternally grateful for your love and support. I can't thank you enough for being "Deb." Without you the chapters of those special years would never have been so wonderful.

Many thanks to my mom for all your thoughtfulness, the notes in our lunch boxes, the newspaper clippings, and all the help with paperwork — from school through trial. Your unconditional love taught me about the bonds between parents and children. Thank you for your constant love, concern, and support. I am blessed to be your son.

Thanks to my dad for always providing the words of wisdom I needed and for still being there when they fell upon deaf ears. You are a wonderful model of doing what needs to be done, of persever-ance, determination, integrity, and humility — all coupled with a quick wit and wonderful sense of humor. It's an honor to be your son.

Thanks to my little sister. I am so glad you are my only sibling — I wouldn't know how to divide the love if I had another. I'll never forget that moment from the witness stand (of all places), when I was so proud to be reminded that indeed blood is thicker than water, always.

Sincere thanks to Nina and Brian Taylor, Editorial Director and Cre-ative Director, respectively, of Pneuma Books. I knew from our first conversations you were going to stick with me and that I should stick with you. With patience, kindness, and professionalism you sifted through my ideas, materials, and shifting directions and helped me deliver just what I wanted. Thank you for all your profession-al guidance.

Thanks to my son's mother, my ex-wife. What's past is past. But, without you, we would not have such a wonderful son and for that, I am eternally grateful. With every end, there is a new beginning.

All my thanks to my precious son, my main man. You will never know exactly how much you mean to me. When you were little and I walked to Big Rock with you in my arms, I think it was re-ally you who carried me. There is no stronger love. Your happiness is my main concern, then, now, and always. I am so proud to be your dad. I love you with all my heart.

About the Author

Mike Mastracci is a founding member and former vice president of the Maryland Collaborative Law Association. He is also a present or past member of the Baltimore City, Baltimore County, and American Bar Associations; Maryland Criminal Defense Association; Maryland Trial Lawyers Association; and the International Association of Collaborative Professionals. Mike also founded and operated the Child Access Center, Inc. in 1998 and 1999, Maryland's only full-service child access center.

Mike Mastracci's own divorce and acrimonious custody battle led to his passion for family law. He writes extensively on the subject on his websites (www.DivorceWithoutDishonor.com, www.StopFightingOverTheKids.com, and www.mikethelawyer.com) and for print publications. He also serves numerous family law clients in his private practice.

Mike graduated from the University of Baltimore School of Law and has been practicing law since 1989 when he joined his father's law firm. He is divorced and remarried and is the proud parent of a teenage son.

Mike believes that parents in divorce situations can manage to amicably resolve differences and establish happy and healthy lifestyles for themselves and their children without fighting in court. Though it may take time, effort, compromise, and sacrifice, he maintains that it is well worth it. Mike is committed to the emotional protection of children of separation and divorce by empowering their parents with the ability to demonstrate that they love their children more than they dislike their ex.

"Mike the Lawyer"

Mike's "Main Man"

You Can Protect
Your Children and Yourself
through a Divorce!

You <u>Can Do It</u> without <u>Dishonor</u>!

For more information about Divorce Without Dishonor —
help, resources, and materials, please visit our website:

www.DivorceWithoutDishonor.com

Spread the Word.

This fine book is available at discount for bulk purchasing
for qualifying instutions and organizations —
such as, libraries; colleges and universities; special collections;
faith-based organizantions; business institutions; associations;
law practices; psychologists and counseling centers;
other individual professionals and as a premium
for incentive programs.

Contact St. Gabriel's Press to get this book into circulation:
info@saintgabrielspress.com
Or visit them online at www.SaintGabrielsPress.com
or www.DivorceWithoutDishonor.com
Office: (410) 869-3400

Available online at:
Amazon, Alibris, and Abe Books

Mike Mastracci is available to write articles for your publication
or website and is available for media interviews
and speaking engagements. Please contact him via email at
info@saintgabrielspress.com

STOP FIGHTING OVER THE KIDS

DivorceWithoutDishonor.com

3585714

Made in the USA